Creative Development

Mavis Brown

Publisher's information

Brilliant Publications
1 Church View
Sparrow Hall Farm
Edlesborough
Dunstable, Bedfordshire
LU6 2ES

Tel: **01525 229720**
Fax: **01525 229725**
e-mail: **sales@brilliantpublications.co.uk**
Website: **www.brilliantpublications.co.uk**

Creative Development by Mavis Brown
Illustrated by Kirsty Brown

© 2002 Mavis Brown

ISBN 1 897675 941

First published in the UK in 2003
10 9 8 7 6 5 4 3 2 1

Printed in Malta by Interprint Ltd.

There are six books in the Foundation Blocks series, one for each of the key areas. Each book contains clearly laid-out pages, giving a wealth of activities, ideas and suggestions. For further details on how these books are structured and how they make implementing the Qualification and Curriculum Authority's *Curriculum Guidance for the Foundation Stage* easy, please see **Introduction** on page 6.

Other books in the Foundation Blocks series are:

Communication, Language and Literacy
by Irene Yates
Encourages children to develop good communication skills, extend their vocabulary, use language to help thinking, begin to link sounds and letters, use and enjoy books, and start to develop writing skills.

Knowledge and Understanding of the World
by Mavis Brown
Provides children with opportunities for early scientific exploration and investigation, and developing skills for design and making. Helps children to experience information and communication technology, develop a sense of time and place, and an awareness of other cultures and beliefs.

Mathematical Development
by Rebecca Taylor
The activities in this book will help children to use numbers, count to 10, recognize numerals to 9, begin to do simple calculations, and start to develop an understanding of shape, space and measures.

Personal, Social and Emotional Development
by Mavis Brown
Helps children to develop positive attitudes, self-confidence and high self-esteem. The activities encourage them to form good relationships with peers and adults; understand what is right, what is wrong and why; and to develop self-care skills with a sense of community.

Physical Development
by Maureen Warner
Encourages children to move with confidence, control and co-ordination, using a variety of equipment. Helps them to gain awareness of space, of themselves and of others, and to recognize the importance of keeping healthy.

Contents

© Mavis Brown
www.brilliantpublications.co.uk

Shapes – Balloons project

Toys – Nutcracker project

Transport and travel – Seaside project

Water – Sorcerer's Apprentice project

Weather – Freezing cold project

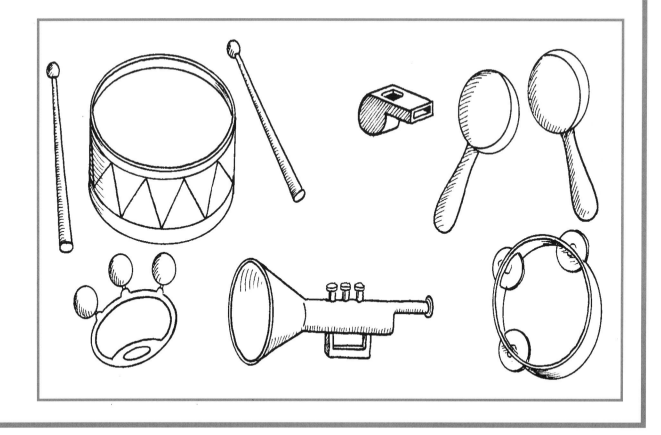

Introduction

- This book has 152 differentiated activities set in real-life contexts relevant to preschool children (3 to 5 years old). It provides coverage of the Creative Development section of the *Curriculum Guidance for the Foundation Stage* (QCA 2000).

- The activities present multi-sensorial creative opportunities through which Early Years practitioners can encourage and support young children to extend their play, develop their own ideas, and communicate them through art, music and dance, role play and imaginative play – giving them effective tools for future learning in visual arts, music, dance and drama.

- The book is divided into four chapters:

Media and Materials (Visual Arts)

- This first chapter concentrates upon skills, techniques and knowledge to be developed before the children create their very own work in response to stimuli in the later chapters.

- Examples of sculptures by well-known artists have not been shown in this book because a photograph offers only a two-dimensional limited viewpoint. A three-dimensional structure needs to be appreciated in its own space by walking round the object to note the quality of the material and its place in space, and to respond to its actual size.

- Photographs of paintings also lack texture and do not show the techniques used, losing most of the communication between the artist and the viewer. It is therefore strongly recommended that the children are taken to an art gallery to see actual works of art.

Music and Dance

- This chapter includes:
  - activities involving singing and making up songs, introducing the concepts of rhyming, rhythm and pitch – all of which help to develop language and reading;
  - activities to help children learn to use percussion instruments and to listen;
  - dance activities to develop body awareness within time and space constraints. Lead-and-follow activities can develop team-building skills;
  - opportunities for all children to present and perform;
  - opportunities to listen to recorded music and to watch videos of performed music and dance.

Imagination

- Play activities should be structured to enhance imaginative play. The activities in this book encourage children to listen to stories and poems, play with small-world toys and puppets made by the children, and dress up and role play in the home corner.

- Encouraging 'What if' scenarios will enable children to verbalize their own ideas. Imaginative people can take ideas and develop them further in time and space. By developing children's ability to see and hear, and even smell and feel, in the 'mind's eye', their imaginative responses to concrete stimuli can be developed and they can then imitate and create stories.

- By joining in with the play as a character, practitioners will encourage imaginative responses from the youngest children and sustain their role play.

© Mavis Brown
www.brilliantpublications.co.uk

- It is important not to over-plan a play activity – otherwise the children's work will not be their own, nor will they be given the opportunity to use their own imagination.

Communication

- This Early Learning goal involves the ability of the children to choose their own method of communicating their response to an experience by drawing together the knowledge, skills and techniques they have mastered in art and design, music and dance, and imaginative and role play.

- In this chapter, therefore, each topic has a theme (eg Seasons has The Selfish Giant project) for which the sheets incorporate activities in each of the creative subject areas. By completing all of the sheets in the theme, the children will have progressed along those stepping stones towards the Early Learning Goals for responding to experiences, and expressing and communicating ideas. The level of difficulty indicated on the sheet refers to the stepping stones for both Communication and the associated creative area (see **Assessment sheets,** pages 10–14).

Creativity

- Each of the creative subjects has its own essential skills, techniques and processes that provide young children with unique insights and ways of assimilating and expressing learning. Through creating, communicating, performing, and responding to art, music, dance, role play and imaginative play children can develop:
  - the ability to think in nonverbal and visual images;
  - the ability to express their ideas and emotions in different symbolic forms and translate them from one form of creativity into another;

- skills to assist in readiness for reading and writing;
- expressive means for self-discovery, their place in their environment and exploration of the world around them;
- motivation, self-confidence, curiosity, independence and persistence;
- cooperative working strategies and respect for the contributions of others;
- an appreciation of the similarities and differences between society today and in the past;
- an appreciation of their own and others' cultural identities.

- To encourage creativity, concentrate on the process, not the outcome, and give the children opportunities to represent their ideas in any of the creative subject areas. The practitioner should provide plenty of materials of good quality and variety, and a wide range of direct experiences to look at, handle and think about to enable the children to practise making connections, choices and comparisons and solving problems for their work to become their own.

Planning

- Each chapter covers the curriculum for Creative Development in the context of sixteen topics commonly used in Early Years and Primary settings. These are:
  - Animals
  - Celebrations
  - Colours
  - Families
  - Food and shopping
  - Gardening
  - Health
  - Homes
  - Myself
  - People who help us
  - Seasons
  - Shapes
  - Toys
  - Transport and travel
  - Water
  - Weather

- The topic appears in a shaded box at the top of each page. The other books in this series also use these same topics. While we have suggested topics, they are not set in concrete. All the activities can easily be modified to fit into a topic of your choice or placed with other topics in this book (see **Topics index**, pages 175–176).
  - ◆ Related activities in the same topic and chapter are not listed as this information can be found in the **Topic index** and **Assessment sheets**.

- All activities include aspects of the Speaking and Listening component of Communication, Language and Literacy. Physical Development and Personal, Social and Emotional Development areas of learning are also included in some activities.

- Prior knowledge is not expected for any of the activities. It is the practitioner's responsibility to choose a suitable activity with the developmental age of the children in mind.

- Each activity begins with an 'energizer' to inspire and motivate the children and kick start their curiosity. Many activities suggest a story, poem, music or painting which can help the children to relate their own experiences and interests to the activity.

- Although plenary sessions have not been included, it is expected that the practitioner will make time to look back and celebrate what the children have done by talking about it. Allow time for them to respond to their peers' work. Encourage them to share their creation and, where appropriate, to refine and rehearse their work for performance.

- The practitioner needs to be mindful that in showing their own ideas the children will be exposing themselves to personal criticism. You will need to be sensitive to this when supporting and encouraging improvement. You can discuss:
  - ◆ what the children were asked to do;
  - ◆ composition, such as use of fantasy or imagination;
  - ◆ techniques used;
  - ◆ use of shapes, colours, lines, patterns, tone, texture and contrasts;
  - ◆ scale, size of design, materials used;
  - ◆ feelings evoked by the artwork;
  - ◆ effort put in.

Logos used on the activity sheets

Box 1 – group size

- This box indicates the number of children recommended for the activity, keeping safety and level of difficulty in mind. Less able children can achieve more difficult tasks with a smaller child-to-adult ratio. The group size indicates the size of group for the activity itself, rather than for any introductory or plenary sessions.

(2–4)

Box 2 – level of difficulty

- This box uses a scale between 1 and 5 to depict the level of difficulty the task might present to the children. 1 indicates an activity suitable for children working in the 'yellow band' of the *Curriculum Guidance for the Foundation Stage;* 5 indicates an activity suitable for able children in the reception class, who are meeting the Early Learning Goals. As most settings have mixed age groups, the majority of the activities have been structured so that the whole class can be involved. Higher levels can be achieved through outcome and the suggested extension activities.

Box 3 – time needed to complete the activity

● The suggested time slots are only a guideline. Children need time to practise their skills, test their ideas and reflect upon their findings. Some children will wish to extend the original activity to pursue their own enquiries or improve upon their creation.

Safety logo

● This symbol (which appears in the Resources box) will alert you that close adult supervision is required. Where relevant, additional safety notes are included on the sheets. You are advised to read these before commencing the activity.

● As young children cannot anticipate danger, all practitioners should be vigilant and take part in a regular risk-assessment exercise relevant to their own setting.

● Any rules issued by your employer or LEA should be adhered to in priority to the recommendations in this book; therefore check your employer's and LEA's Health and Safety guidelines and their policies on the use of equipment and visits out of the setting.

Links to home

● The word *parent* is used to refer to any person responsible for the child, and can include mothers, fathers, legal guardians and primary carers of children in public care. The 'Links to home' suggest ways in which carers can continue and reinforce the learning that is experienced at the setting.

● Parents can give important information about the children and their experiences on which the practitioner can

build. It is essential that the practitioner is informed of any health problems, in particular of any allergies.

● Parents can be a valuable resource by giving support when extra help is needed during visits out of the setting, and with more complex activities.

● Resources including 'recycled materials' can often be supplied by parents.

Display

● It is important to display children's work as it adds value and worth to their endeavours.

● If your setting has a multiple use or limited wall area, negotiate with managers of the premises for extra wall space. Wall displays can go on a hardboard sheet, or display panels, which can be folded and put away. The collections can be kept in a labelled accessible box. Work can also be hung from a washing line across the room (high enough not to be a hazard) or from the ceiling from wire clothes hangers as mobiles. Work can also be attached to draped fabric.

● **Individual work** – Mount on black paper, with a margin of 10–20mm, with the top and bottom edges level or symmetrical. (Coloured or patterned mounting paper can detract from the work.) Leave space round each piece of work. Don't overcrowd but let the whole display have balance.

● **Group activity mural** – Give each child a section of the picture to work on. Emphasize the background in a picture with black silhouettes. Use different techniques to give depth, eg: collage, painting, printing.

Assessment sheets

Assessment

- Each activity has learning objectives which are linked to the Creative Development curriculum.

- To assist the practitioner in the task of planning a balanced programme of experiences, the charts on the following pages show which activities address which of the QCA stepping stones. The charts will also be useful for short-term planning, identifying future learning priorities and ascertaining whether support is required to achieve a level. The comments column can be used to record comments on the group as a whole or on individual children. These sheets may be photocopied.

- Other evidence of the child's achievements in the form of (dated) early writing, dictations, drawings, paintings and photographs of 3D work can be kept in a portfolio. This album can also be a source of celebration and pleasure to look at in the future for the child and parent.

- These records should be retained for inspection.

Curriculum Guidance levels: 　Yellow　　Blue　　Green　　E L G　(Early Learning Goals)

Stepping stone	Activities which address stepping stone	Comments
Begin to differentiate colours	Time to go home; Make a rainbow	
Use their bodies to explore texture and space	Kinara for Kwanzaa; Storm; I don't use these now; Badges; Peaches; Seashells	
Make three-dimensional structures	Fruitful; Tooth fairy beads; Rats	
Differentiate marks and movements on paper	Mehendi hand; Coloured balloons	
Begin to describe the texture of things	Porridge; Peachy tart	
Use lines to enclose a space, then begin to use these shapes to represent objects	Bird masks; Bananananana, Incy wincy spider; Washing line	

Stepping stone	Activities which address stepping stone	Comments
Begin to construct stacking blocks vertically and horizontally and making enclosures and creating spaces	Bricks	
Explore what happens when they mix colours	Coloured shapes; Add water	
Understand that different media can be combined	Spring flowers; Who's broken my chair?	
Make constructions, collages, paintings, drawings and dances	Noah's animals; A lady scarecrow; Wiggly worms; Sick	
Use ideas involving fitting, overlapping, in, out, grids and sun like shapes	Portraits; Hats; Toy soldiers; Mkeka tablemat; Framed wedding; Wedding cake; Dancing clown	
Choose particular colours to use for a purpose	Atishoo; Autumn leaves; I feel ill	
Experiment to create different textures	Tiles; Toast	
Work creatively on a large or small scale	See activities in Communication chapter	
Explore colour, texture, shape, form and space in two or three dimensions	Paper-making; Myself; Lines; Favourite meal; My favourite things; A load of rubbish; Blossom; Icicles; Freezing	
Join in favourite songs	Quiet as a mouse; Family fingers; Baby games	
Show an interest in the way musical instruments sound	What is a dad?; In the mood; Pop	
Respond to sound with body movement	Statues; The red balloon	
Enjoy joining in with dancing and ring games	Ring around; Beside the seaside	
Sing a few simple, familiar songs	Quiet as a mouse; Today's weather; Washing line; Getting colder	

Stepping stone	Activities which address stepping stone	Comments
Sing to themselves and make up simple songs	Sing to your pet; Sing a song of soap; Tra-la	
Tap out simple repeated rhythms and make some up	Rattle those pans; Tick tock; Trains; Zulu music; Marching soldiers; Splish drip splosh	
Explore and learn how sounds can be changed	Plant pots; Bedtime; Dee daw; Fast food	
Imitate and create movement in response to music	Noah's music; Rockin' robin; Reflections; Slow as a snail	
Begin to build a repertoire of songs	Gardening songs; Bobbing boats; Knock, knock	
Explore the different sounds of instruments	Hum and click; My body; The park in the dark	
Begin to move rhythmically	Running water; Piping music; Musical colours; Marching soldiers; The Nutcracker Ballet	
Recognize and explore how sounds can be changed, sing simple songs from memory, recognize repeated sounds and sound patterns and match movement to music	Peter and the Wolf; Hot cross buns; Blue boy; The four seasons; Hip hip hooray; Musical toys; Outer space; Today's weather; Here comes the bride; Gargle; I feel ill; The three bears; The giant's garden; South Pole	
Pretend that one object represents another, especially when objects have characteristics in common	Paint the town red; Shop till you drop; My home	
Notice what adults do, imitating what is observed and then doing it spontaneously when the adult is not there	Hello Grandma; Crossing the road; A nice cup of tea; Hamelin; Not fussy	

Creative Development

Stepping stone	Activities which address stepping stone	Comments
Use one object to represent another, even when the objects have few characteristics in common	Pebble pet; The Selfish Giant; Silly balloons	
Use available resources to create props to support role play	Teddy's birthday party; Messing about in boats; Teddy is ill	
Develop a repertoire of actions by putting a sequence of movements together	Dicing with colour; A bear hunt; Under my umbrella; I don't believe you; Incy wincy spider; Marching soldiers	
Enjoy stories based on themselves and people and places they know well	Grandad's visit; When I was a baby	
Engage in imaginative and role play based on own first-hand experiences	Moving house; What to wear; A day to remember; The beach	
Introduce a story line or narrative into their play	Stuck up the chimney; Losing a tooth; How will Teddy get there?	
Play alongside other children who are engaged in the same theme	Down at the farm; Homes for creepy crawlies	
Play cooperatively as part of a group to act out a narrative	Soup for sale!; Break in; I want to be ...	
Use their imagination in art and design, music, dance, imaginative play, role play and stories	Fantastic animals; What has eaten the lettuce?; Baked beans; Decorate a tree; Eat your greens; My imaginary life; Trees; Growing plants; Clowns; Are we there yet?; Windy weather; Over the rainbow; Monster insects; Too full	
Show an interest in what they see, hear, smell, touch and feel	Rats; Make a rainbow; I don't use these now; Baby games; Badges; Peaches; Pop; The red balloon; Seashells	
Use body language, gestures, facial expression or words to indicate personal satisfaction or frustration	Hamelin; Not fussy; Beside the seaside	

Stepping stone	Activities which address stepping stone	Comments
Further explore an experience using a range of senses	Zulu music; Incy wincy spider; Slow as a snail; Teddy is ill; Peachy tart; Coloured balloons; Marching soldiers; Splish drip splosh	
Begin to use representation as a means of communication	Fast food; When I was a baby; Silly balloons; The beach; Getting colder	
Describe experiences and past actions, using a widening range of materials	I don't believe you; The Selfish Giant; Washing line	
Try to capture experiences and responses with music, dance, paint and other materials or words	Piping music; A lady scarecrow; Musical colours; A day to remember; Toast; Wiggly worms; Sick; Break in; Knock, knock	
Develop preferences for forms of expression	Goldilocks and the three bears; The Sorcerer's Apprentice	
Talk about personal intentions, describing what they were trying to do	Mkeka tablemat; Wedding cake; Incy wincy spider; Who's broken my chair?	
Respond to comments and questions, entering into dialogue about their creations	Framed wedding; Sandcastles	
Make comparisons	I want to be ...; Dancing clown; The Nutcracker Ballet	
Respond in a variety of ways to what they see, hear, smell, touch and feel	Kwanzaa; My favourite things; Blossom; Only a dream	
Express and communicate their ideas, thoughts and feelings by using a widening range of materials and suitable tools, imaginative and role play, movement, designing and making, and a variety of songs and musical instruments	Pied Piper of Hamelin; Over the rainbow; Here comes the bride; Favourite meal; Monster insects; Gargle; I feel ill; The three bears; A load of rubbish; The giant's garden; Too full; Icicles; South Pole; Freezing	

Creative Development

© Mavis Brown
www.brilliantpublications.co.uk

Noah's animals

Media and Materials

• • • • • • • • • •

Resources
- Book: *Professor Noah's Spaceship* by Brian Wildsmith (Oxford University Press)
- Books and photographs of male and female animals
- Music: *Carnival of Animals* suite by Camille Saint-Saëns (1835–1921)
- CD player
- Paint or crayons as required
- Paintbrushes
- Stiff cardboard animal masks
- Elastic
- Stapler
- Scissors

• • • • • • • • • •

 Supervise the use of scissors and staplers

Learning objectives
- To make constructions, collages and dances
- To colour in masks with the appropriate colours

Preparation
- Draw or copy animal face masks.

What to do
Circle time
- Read a story about Noah, eg *Professor Noah's Spaceship*.
- Suggest that the children make masks so that they can role play the story.
- With the children, list the animals in the story.
- Show photographs of the animals. What animal is this? Is it the male or the female? Support language development: *lion, lioness, bull, cow, ram, ewe.*

Art activity
- Let each child choose an animal face mask to cut out.
- Ask what colours they should use. Ask the child to find a picture of the animal in the book corner.
- Support colouring in the masks. Help the children to tie elastic through the holes on the side.

Extension/variation
- Perform *Professor Noah's Spaceship* while dancing to *Carnival of Animals*.

Links to home
- Ask for help with cutting and colouring the masks.
- Invite parents to watch the performance of *Professor Noah's Spaceship*.

Related activities
- Noah's music (see page 42)
- Rats (see page 105)

8

Bird masks

Learning objective

(8)
- To make a bird mask with a beak

What to do

- Cut out mask for face. Attach elastic.

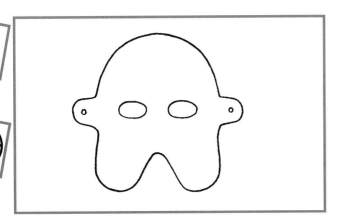

- With practitioner's support, cut shape for beak as shown.
- Fold to flex into beak shape.

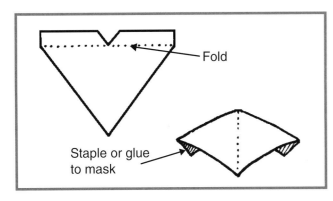

Fold

Staple or glue to mask

- Attach beak to face mask with staples. Cover staples with sticky tape.

- Paint and decorate mask.

Extension/variation

- Use the bird masks with Noah's animals (see page 15).

Related activities

- Noah's music (see page 42)
- Rockin' robin (see page 45)
- Rats (see page 105)
- The Selfish Giant project (see pages 145–150)

Resources

■ Paint or crayons as required
■ Paintbrushes
■ Elastic
■ Simple bird mask made from stiff card
■ Stiff card, eg: cereal box
■ Sticky tape
■ Stapler
■ Scissors

⚠ Supervise the use of scissors and staplers.

© Mavis Brown
www.brilliantpublications.co.uk

Mehendi hand

Media and Materials

• • • • • • • • •

Resources

- Photocopies of drawings of hand with patterns marked on them with dotted lines
- Brown or dark red crayon or pencil
- Internet: www.mehendiart.com

Learning objective
● To draw mehendi hand patterns

Preparation
● Prepare copies of patterns on outline of hand.

What to do

Circle time
● Explain that the day before a Hindu girl gets married her girl friends and family decorate her hands and feet with a red plant dye called henna or mehendi.
● The bride's wedding designs usually include the groom's name hidden amongst the patterns on her palm.

Art activity
● Trace round the shapes on the outline of the hand.

Extension/variation
● The child writes their name on the drawing of the hand, then draws round the name to hide it. (Do not draw over the name.)

Related activities
● Wedding project (see pages 117–120)

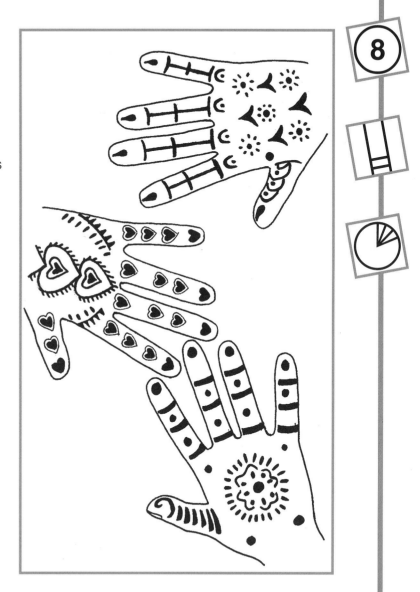

Kinara for Kwanzaa

Learning objective
- To make a candle holder (*Kinara*) for the festival of Kwanzaa

Preparation
- Wedge the clay to remove air in preparation.

Notes for practitioners
- The festival of Kwanzaa, celebrated during the seven days between 26th December and 1st January, was created to celebrate and strengthen the family, community and culture of African-American people as well as Africans throughout the world through the seven basic principles or values (*Nguzo Saba*). These are: Unity (*Umoja*), Self-Determination (*Kujichagulia*), Collective Work and Responsibility (*Ujima*), Cooperative Economics (*Ujamaa*), Purpose (*Nia*), Creativity (*Kuumba*) and Faith (*Imani*).
- Kwanzaa has seven basic symbols and two supplemental ones.

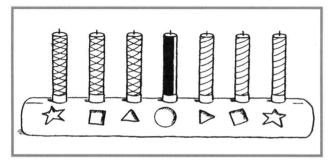

What to do
Circle time
- Explain simply the festival of Kwanzaa.
- The *Kinara* is symbolic of life and holds seven candles, *Mishumaa Saba*, which represent the seven principles. One candle is lit each day of the festival. The central black candle is lit first, then alternate red and green (red candles on one side, green together on the other).

Craft activity
- Support making the *Kinara* and use appropriate language, eg 'shape', 'decorate'.
- Roll the clay into a fat sausage shape. Talk about the texture and shape of the clay.
- Flatten the sides and base so that it is stable.
- Push the seven candles with holders into the clay. Make sure it balances.
- Decorate the outside of the clay by pressing in shapes.
- After the *Kinara* has hardened, paint in red, black and green colours.

Extension/variation
- Playdough (see page 29) could be used instead of clay, but this may not withstand heat.

Links to home
- Ask for helpers with the craft work.

Related activities
- Kwanzaa project (see pages 109–112)

Resources
- Modelling clay suitable to withstand the heat from a candle
- Red, black and green paint
- Knife for cutting clay
- Rolling pin
- Tools to make patterns in clay
- Birthday cake candles: 1 black, 3 red, 3 green
- 7 candle holders
- Internet: www.officialkwanzaa website.org

 Close supervision is required when using real candles. Keep the matches on your person at all times. Check that the clay can withstand the heat from the candle before use.

Creative Development

Time to go home

Media and Materials

● ● ● ● ● ● ● ● ● ●

Resources
■ No special requirements

Learning objectives
● To begin to differentiate colours
● To begin to describe the texture of things

What to do
Circle time
● The children sit in a circle.
● The practitioner chooses groups of children to put on their coats by describing the colour/texture of what they are wearing. For example, the children who are wearing red can put their coats on. The person who is wearing a fluffy jumper, etc.
● Ask the children to feel their clothes and describe the texture.

Extension/variation
● Let the children take turns in choosing the colours.

Links to home
● Ask parents to reinforce the names of colours.

Related activity
● My home (see page 89)

© Mavis Brown
www.brilliantpublications.co.uk

Creative Development   **19**

Coloured shapes

Learning objective
- To explore mixing colours and make a picture in the style of Josef Albers

Preparation
- Access paint program on the computer.

What to do
Circle time
- Show the painting *Study for Homage to the Square: Beaming* (1963), which comprises three overlying squares of decreasing size. The colours of the squares are blue, blue-green and green.

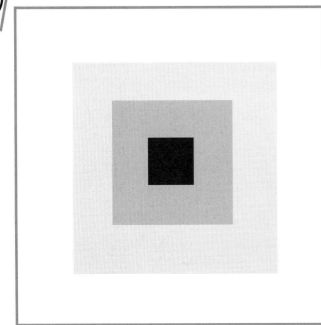

Art activity
- Choose two of the primary colours (red, blue, yellow).
- Starting with one colour, paint a square.
- Add a small amount of the second colour and paint another square.
- Continue adding the second colour and paint new squares.
- Paint the last square in the second colour only.
- Choose three painted squares.
- Cut or tear into three different sized squares.
- Stick the squares on top of each other in decreasing size.

Extensions/variations
- Choose any shape and treat the same as above.
- Use different painting tools including fingers.
- Use the paint program on the computer.

Related activities
- Paper-making (see page 24–25)
- Tiles (see page 36)
- Lines (see page 38)
- What has eaten the lettuce? (see page 79)

Media and Materials

• • • • • • • • •

Resources
- Painting: *Study for Homage to the Square: Beaming* (1963) by Josef Albers (1888–1976)
- Paints - red, blue and yellow
- Paintbrushes
- Paper
- Glue and spreader
- Scissors
- Computer with paint program, eg *2simple Infant Video Toolkit* (2simple Software) and printer and paper

• • • • • • • • •

 Supervise the use of scissors.

Portraits

Media and Materials

• • • • • • • • • •

Resources
- Paintings: *Mr and Mrs Andrews* (1750) by Thomas Gainsborough (1727–1788); *Mr and Mrs Clark and Percy* (1970) by David Hockney (b.1937)
- Camera and tripod
- Film for camera (to be loaded as part of the activity)
- Dressing-up clothes
- Coloured cloths for background
- Paints
- Paintbrushes
- Paper

Learning objective
- To photograph or paint a portrait of two people

What to do
Circle time
- Show the two paintings of husband and wife.
- Ask what clues they see in the expressions and gestures of the people that determine their relationship.
- Ask why the portraits were made, eg to make a record of an important time in their life, to show that they are wealthy.
- Talk about what the people in the paintings are wearing, the painted surroundings and colours used to give help with the children's ideas.
- Ask about the composition: are the people standing or sitting? (Hockney's friends include their cat in the portrait.)
- Ask what they feel about the people in the paintings.
- Ask how they could record a portrait (photograph).
- Ask two children wearing dressing-up clothes to replicate a portrait.

Art activity
- Open up a camera and show how a film is loaded into it.
- Support the taking of photographs.
- Discuss the composition of their photograph, eg background, figures, pose, expression, character, colour of clothes, favourite objects.
- Discuss whether the resulting picture will tell what they are trying to convey.

Extension/variation
- Paint a family portrait.

Related activities
- Wedding project (see pages 117–120)

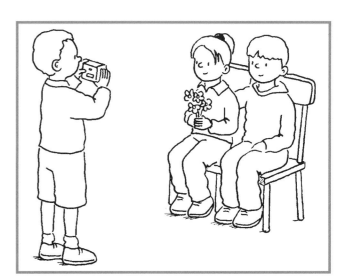

Porridge

Learning objective

4
- To explore and begin to describe the texture of things

What to do

Circle time
- Read the story of *Goldilocks and the Three Bears*. Suggest that the children make some porridge.

Cooking activity
- Let the child do the measuring and stirring.
- Put porridge oats into the casserole dish. Ask how the porridge feels as well as looks (eg soft, makes a scrunchy noise when rubbed together).
- Add water and milk and stir. Ask if the porridge dissolves (no).
- Cook in a microwave oven at 850W for three minutes. An adult should remove the porridge from the microwave.
- Stir and return to oven for two more minutes.
- Ask what the porridge looks like now. Stir the cooked porridge.

Snack time
- Serve and add milk and sweetener as required.

Extensions/variations
- Make some porridge too sweet or too salty.
- Encourage a role play conversation between the children as if they are the bears or Goldilocks as they eat the porridge.

Related activities
- Goldilocks project (see pages 133–136)
- Peachy tart (see page 147)

Media and Materials

• • • • • • • • •

Resources
- Book: *Goldilocks and the Three Bears* (Ladybird does a nice edition)

For 3 or 4 portions of porridge
- 1 cup porridge oats
- 1 cup water
- 1 cup milk
- Milk to add
- Sugar or syrup
- Salt
- Teaspoon
- Glass casserole dish with lid
- Wooden spoon
- Cup or beaker
- Cereal dishes
- Spoons
- Microwave oven

• • • • • • • • •

 Check records for diabetes. Although the microwave oven does not feel hot, the heat from the porridge will be conducted to the glass.

Media and Materials

● ● ● ● ● ● ● ● ●

Resources
- Poem: 'Banananananananana' by William Cole, from *The Orchard Book of Funny Poems* (Orchard)
- Fruits and vegetables
- Pale coloured chalks
- Coloured wax crayons
- Candle
- Water colours
- Water-based black ink or dark coloured dye
- Paintbrush
- Paper towel
- White paper
- Scissors

● ● ● ● ● ● ● ● ●

 Supervise the use of scissors.

Learning objective
● To make a picture using chalk and crayon resist

What to do

Circle time
● Read the poem and show the fruits and vegetables.
● Ask for names of fruits and extend the word eg *peachchchch*, *plummmm*. Encourage everyone to say the words.

Art activity
● Explain to the children that they will be making special chalk and crayon resist pictures of fruits and vegetables.
● Encourage them to try out ideas on small sheets of paper first.
● Write the word and draw shapes of the fruits and vegetables several times over the paper using the chalk thickly.
● Thickly colour in round the drawings and words with different coloured wax crayons, leaving no paper showing.
● Support brushing the ink or dye over the whole picture. The chalk should suck up the ink, and the wax resist it.
● Support mopping off excess ink with the paper towel.
● The children could trim the paper to the shape of the fruit or vegetable for display.

Extension/variation
● Write words using a candle, then draw lines across the page. Colour using water colours which will shrink from the wax.

Links to home
● Ask parents to reinforce names of fruits and vegetables.

Related activity
● Fruitful (see page 26)

8

Paper-making

Learning objective
②
● To make recycled paper

Preparation
Making mould and deckle
● Stretch net curtain over the flat face of one of the frames and pin in place on the underside. This is your mould.
● The other frame will be your deckle. It sits on top and is held firmly in place by hand.

Making pressing boards
● Drill a hole in each corner of the two sheets of plywood for the bolts, at least 2cm in from the edge.

What to do
Circle time
● Show the children examples of recycled paper and packaging. Discuss why it is a good idea to use recycled paper items. Suggest to the children that they make their own recycled paper. Show the mould, deckle and pressing boards and explain what is going to happen.

Art activity
● At each stage discuss the appearance and texture of the material.

Day one
● Let the children tear 50g of clean scrap paper (envelope paper with blue inside is excellent) and put it into the bowl.
● Away from the children pour on 750ml boiling water.

● When the mixture is cool show it to the children. Let it soak overnight.

Day two
● Let children add 1 tablespoon of PVA glue and 1 large yoghurt pot of water to the soaked paper. (Note: 500g yoghurt pot contains about 400ml water.)
● Let the children take turns to stir the mixture with a wooden spoon.
● Away from children macerate the mixture in a blender.

Day three – pulp bath
● Work next to a sink but take care to prevent any paper going down the drain.
● Half fill a large rectangular washing-up bowl with water and let the children add 6 x 500g yoghurt pots full of blended pulp.
● One child stirs mixture up and down (not round and round) with wooden spoon.
● A second child grips the mould with the deckle on top, and plunges them down vertically at the far end of the bowl (deckle facing the child), slides them horizontally along the bottom, then lifts them vertically to the surface of the liquid.
● The water runs through the net, leaving a layer of pulped paper on top of the net. Wait a few seconds for it to drain.
● Place the mould flat in the sink and carefully lift the deckle vertically off the mould.

Media and Materials
• • • • • • • • • •
Resources
Mould and deckle
■ 2 identical small flat wooden picture frames
■ Net curtain
■ Drawing pins

Pressing boards
■ 2 sheets four-ply plywood
■ 4 long bolts with wing nuts
■ Drill and bit (slightly larger than bolts)

Pulp bath
■ Kitchen scales
■ 50g clean scrap paper (not newspaper)
■ Large rectangular washing-up bowl
■ 750ml boiling water
■ 1 tablespoon PVA glue
■ 500g yoghurt pot
■ 400ml cold water
■ Wooden spoon
■ Electric blender (for use by practitioner)
■ Large container for pulp
■ Plastic aprons

For circle time
■ Samples of recycled paper and packaging materials

Media and Materials

• • • • • • • • • •

Resources

For pressing
- 2 old towels
- 30 rectangles of kitchen cloth (not paper towels) slightly larger size than mould
- Sponge
- Scissors
- Pressing board
- Flowers
- Leaves
- Fabric pieces
- Kitchen cloth with different surface

For drying
- Clothes line
- Pegs

• • • • • • • • • •

Place line high enough not to catch children. Supervise the use of scissors.

Day three – pressing
- Place one folded towel on top of one of the pressing boards. This will be the bottom of the pile.
- Place a clean kitchen cloth on top of the towel. Turn the mould over on to the cloth.
- Press over the paper with a sponge to remove water. The paper should stick to the cloth. Roll off the mould.
- You can add pressed flowers or leaves at this stage on top of the paper or change the texture by lying material with a different surface on top. Add another sheet of kitchen cloth.
- Plunge the mould into the pulp bath again to make another sheet of paper. When you have made as much paper as you want, place a second towel on the top of the pile of kitchen cloths-and-paper sandwich and place the second board on top.
- Screw the boards together, tightening the wing nuts, and leave overnight or longer.

Day four
- After pressing, separate the cloths. With the paper still attached to them, hang the cloths out on a line to dry.

Day five
- The paper should now be dry. Peel the paper from the cloth.
- This paper can be written on with felt-tip pens and pen, or can be used in collages or cards.

Extensions/variations
- Thin paper can be used to wrap presents.
- Thick paper can be used to make greetings cards.
- Make different coloured recycled paper and use in collages.

Related activities
- Coloured shapes (see page 20)
- Teddy's birthday party (see page 75)
- A load of rubbish (see page 144)

Fruitful

• • • • • • • • • •

(6)

Learning objectives
● To make fruits and vegetables from papier-mâché pulp
● To paint with appropriate colours

What to do
Circle time
● Pass round the whole fruit and vegetables.
● Let the children examine them and describe what they see, smell and feel.
● Cut up the fruit and vegetables and let the children see what they look like inside.
● Let the children taste the food and ask them whether they like it.
● Support language development for colour, texture, size, shape and taste, and names and parts of the fruit and vegetables.
● Read *Oliver's Vegetables* or *Oliver's Fruit Salad*.

Art activity
● Support moulding the papier mâché pulp into the correct shapes for fruit and vegetables.
● Cover the shapes with white tissue paper.
● Allow to dry then paint in the appropriate colour.

Extensions/variations
● Display the African fruit and vegetables in the basket for the Kwanzaa feast (see page 112).
● Peach fruit made in this way could be used for The Selfish Giant project.

Links to home
● Ask parents to talk about the names of vegetables and if they grow on top of the ground or in the soil.
● Ask parents to talk about the names of fruits and how they develop from flowers.

Related activities
● Bananananana (see page 23)
● Kwanzaa project (see pages 109–112)
● The Selfish Giant project (see pages 145–150)

■ Samples of vegetables and fruits, including a peach, and examples from Africa
■ Knife and cutting board for practitioner
■ Bin
■ Kitchen towels
■ Newspaper pulp made from pieces of torn newspaper with wallpaper glue (without fungicide)
■ Tray
■ Thin white tissue paper
■ Paintbrushes
■ Ready-mixed paints in suitable colours for fruits and vegetables
■ Wicker basket for display
■ Books: *Oliver's Vegetables* and *Oliver's Fruit Salad* by Vivian French (Hodder Children's Books)

• • • • • • • • • •

 Always check on allergies.

Atishoo

Media and Materials

• • • • • • • • •

Resources

- White cotton handkerchiefs
- Fabric dyes for use in washing machine
- Cooking salt
- Lots of smooth pebbles
- Balls of string
- Washing machine, tumble drier, iron
- Wooden clothes pegs

• • • • • • • • • •

 As the tie-dyeing is done in the washing machine, this should not be hazardous. Supervise the children when using the washing machine and tumble drier. Keep children away from the iron and talk about safety.

Learning objective

- To tie-dye a handkerchief to make a sneeze pattern

What to do

Craft activity
Tie-dyeing

- Cotton will dye brighter colours than will polyester cotton fabric.
- Cold water dyes can be used, but they are not so bright, and buckets of dye wash have to be kept somewhere.
- Wrap a pebble in the handkerchief, twisting it into a ball. Tie the pebble tightly in place.

- Follow instructions on the dye packet, putting the salt and dye in the drum of the washing machine.
- After washing and drying, iron the handkerchiefs.
- The pattern should look like a sneeze!

Extensions/variations

- Tie in a second pebble and use a second colour.

4

- Try different ways of tying the fabric, eg use clothes pegs. Compare the patterns.
- Use red, green and black colours and make a tablecloth for the Kwanzaa celebrations.
- Use dyed fabrics to decorate costumes and hats.

Links to home

- Ask for help with the tying of knots and dyeing.

Related activities

- Pied Piper project (see pages 105–108)
- Kwanzaa project (see pages 109–112)
- The Selfish Giant project (see pages 145–150)

Tooth fairy beads

Learning objective
● To make beads for a necklace

Preparation
● This activity is best done in conjunction with one or more of the children losing a tooth.

What to do

Circle time
● Read one of the books.
● Talk about losing a tooth, and the tooth fairy using the teeth that have fallen out to make jewellery.
● Look at the shapes of the teeth.
● Talk about the size of the fairies, and how the teeth will seem large.

Craft activity
● Shape 'teeth' from playdough (see page 29).
● Support using a cocktail stick to make holes in the beads. Twist the stick as the playdough dries.
● Remove the stick before baking the beads.
● Paint with white paint, and allow to dry.
● Thread the beads together to make a necklace.

Extension/variation
● Colour the beads red, black and green for the Kwanzaa celebrations.

Related activities
● Losing a tooth (see page 87)
● Kwanzaa project (see pages 109–112)

Media and Materials

● ● ● ● ● ● ● ● ● ●

Resources
■ Book: *Dave and the Tooth Fairy* by Verna Allette Wilkins (Tamarind Books)
■ Book: *How Many Teeth?* by Paul Showers (HarperCollins Children's Books) – alternative title
■ Playdough
■ White paint
■ Paintbrushes
■ Cocktail sticks
■ Pictures of teeth
■ False teeth
■ Real baby teeth if available
■ Thread
■ Bodkin

● ● ● ● ● ● ● ● ● ●

⚠ Supervise the use of sharp implements.

© Mavis Brown
www.brilliantpublications.co.uk

Media and Materials

• • • • • • • • • •

Equipment

- Metal spoon
- Tablespoon
- Wooden spoon
- Mixing bowl
- Nonstick saucepan
- Nonstick baking tray
- Oven
- Poster paints
- PVA glue
- Paintbrushes
- Airtight plastic container

Ingredients for salt dough recipe

- 2 cups of plain flour
- 1 cup cooking salt
- 2 tablespoons cream of tartar
- 2 tablespoons cooking oil
- 3/4 cup cold water
- Food colouring (optional)

Ingredients for corn-based recipe

- 1 cup cornflour
- 2 cups bicarbonate of soda
- 1 cup warm water
- Food colouring in the water (optional)

Playdough recipes

To be made by the practitioner:

Salt dough recipe (wheat based)

- Mix salt, flour and cream of tartar together.
- Add oil, then water, mixing well. If colour is needed, add food colouring to the water first.
- Put into saucepan, and boil for 60 seconds, stirring all the time with a wooden spoon. It should form a ball.
- Remove from pan and knead until smooth.
- Cool and store in an airtight plastic tub. It should keep for two weeks.
- Items made from playdough can be baked. Place them on a baking tray and cook for 2 hours on 125°C/250°F/Gas Mark 1.
- The baked dough can be painted with poster paints mixed with a little PVA glue.

If any child is allergic to wheat make corn dough:

Corn dough recipe

- Mix the ingredients together, then boil in the saucepan.
- Cool then knead until smooth.
- This playdough dries fairly quickly in air without baking.
- Store in an airtight container.

(6)

Bricks

. . . .

(4)

Learning objective
● To make a model home from construction bricks

What to do
Circle time
● Read *The Three Little Pigs.* Ask the children whether their home is made from bricks or wood.
● Ask the children to describe their home. Support language development: *storey, roof, wall, door, window, chimney, central heating.*
● Make references to the wall display.

Construction activity
● Ask the children to build a home using the construction bricks.
● Talk with the children about what they are making. Encourage the construction of walls and a roof.

Extension/variation
● Ask them how the bricks are arranged in the wall. Look at a wall outside if possible, and copy the pattern.

Related activities
● Lines (see page 38)
● Stuck up the chimney (see page 76)

Resources
■ Book: *The Three Little Pigs* (Ladybird does a nice edition)
■ Wall display: photographs of homes in different environments (city, town, countryside, suburban), and of different styles (flat, maisonette, bungalow, semi-detached, detached, terraced) and from different ages (Tudor timber-framed, Georgian with sash windows, Victorian terrace, present day estate house)
■ Construction bricks and base

Myself

Media and Materials

• • • • • • • • • •

Resources

- Book: *All Kinds of People* by Emma Damon (Tango)
- Book: *Looking at Paintings: Children* by Peggy Roalf (Belitha Press)
- Plastic mirror
- Balloons
- Vaseline
- Newspaper
- Recycled paper, eg envelopes
- Wallpaper paste (without fungicide)
- Brushes
- White lining paper
- Masking tape
- Coloured wool
- Plasticine
- Stiff cardboard
- Scissors, stapler
- Thick paint and paintbrushes
- Chicken wire

• • • • • • • • • •

 Supervise the use of scissors and staplers.

Learning objective

- To use papier-mâché to make a puppet head representing themselves

What to do

Circle time

- Read *All Kinds of People*. Ask if everyone looks the same.
- Pass the mirror round the circle. Support language development as each child says the colour of their eyes, hair and skin, and type of hair (*curly, straight, long, short*).
- Identify ways in which the children in the class are similar to and different from each other. Challenge any racist remarks.

Art activity

- Explain to the children that they are going to make papier-mâché heads of themselves.
- Help the children to smear vaseline on the balloon to stop the paper sticking to it.
- Using the wallpaper paste, stick small pieces of paper to the balloon. Alternate layers of newspaper and coloured paper to ensure even layers.
- Add relief features (nose, ears) using twisted paper or Plasticine. Discuss how the raised features should be attached.
- Use white lining paper for the last layer.
- When dry, pop the balloon and attach a cylindrical card collar to stand the head on.
- Paint the head and face.
- Add wool as hair.

Book corner

- Look at *Looking at Paintings: Children*. Ask about the clothes worn, the poses and the activities shown.
- If they painted their own portrait, ask what clothes they would be wearing and what they would be doing. Would they show their toys or pet?

Extensions/variations

- Paint self-portraits.
- Make a large head of the giant for The Selfish Giant project with every child contributing. Make a head shape support (armature) using chicken wire.

Related activities

- Portraits (see page 21)
- Hats (see page 32)
- The Selfish Giant project (see pages 145–150)
- Balloons project (see pages 151–154)

(6)

Hats

Learning objective
- To make hats using ideas involving fitting, overlapping, balance, shape and form

Preparation
- Cut out some brims, peaks and round flat shapes for younger children.

What to do
Circle time
- Read *ABC I Can Be* and/or *What Am I?*
- Most people who help us wear special hats. Ask children to describe hats of police, firefighters, the lollipop person, etc.
- Suggest that the children copy a hat, or design one of their own, for someone who helps us.

Craft activity
- Encourage the children to think about which materials suit the character.
- Select the style of hat–cap or helmet (see page 33).
- Support the children in making a hat to fit to their head. Paint or cover with coloured materials.
- Ask the children whether their finished hat balances and fits, and if they have achieved their designed intentions.

Extensions/variations
- Let younger children decorate an existing hat.
- Make hats for the Pied Piper project and the Wedding project. Encourage the children to add a range of materials appropriate to the character. Discuss the qualities and use of: fabrics, yarns, ribbons, foil, papers, tissue paper, artificial flowers, beads, sequins, feathers, tassels and fringes, and paint.

Links to home
- Ask if the setting could borrow some hats to decorate or copy.

Related activities
- Myself (see page 31) for using papier-mâché
- Pied Piper project (pages 105–108)
- Wedding project (pages 117–120)

Media and Materials

• • • • • • • • • •

Resources
- Book: *ABC I Can Be* by Verna Allette Wilkins and Zoë Gorham (Tamarind Books)
- Book: *What Am I?* by Debbie MacKinnon and Anthea Sieveking (Frances Lincoln)
- Photographs of people who help us, showing their hats

For making hats
- Small plates for templates
- Card from cereal boxes
- Crêpe paper
- PVA glue and spreaders
- Sticky tape
- Round balloons
- Wallpaper paste in tray (no fungicide)
- Newspaper
- White lining paper
- Coloured paper, or paint and paintbrushes
- Scissors

• • • • • • • • • •

 Supervise the use of scissors.

Media and Materials

• • • • • • • • • •

Resources
- Hats from dressing-up box

To decorate hats
- Paint and paintbrushes
- Fabrics, yarns, ribbons, foil, coloured papers, tissue paper, artificial flowers, beads, sequins, feathers, tassels and fringes
- PVA glue and spreaders
- Scissors and pinking shears
- Thread and bodkins

• • • • • • • • • •

Supervise the use of sharp tools.

For helmets eg fireman

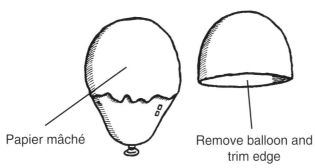
Papier mâché

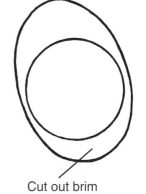
Remove balloon and trim edge

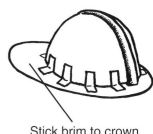
Cut out brim

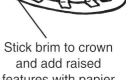
Stick brim to crown and add raised features with papier mâché

6

For caps eg policeman

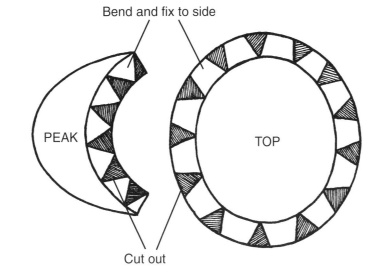
Bend and fix to side

PEAK

TOP

Cut out

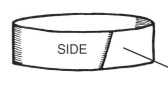
SIDE

For soft cap use crêpe paper for side. For hard cap use stiff card

Spring flowers

Learning objectives

(4)
- To compare paintings of vases of flowers
- To make a two- or three-dimensional representation of a vase of flowers

What to do

Circle time

- Show two different paintings of a vase of flowers. Ask whether the paintings look dark or light.
- How many colours are used? Ask the children to point to the colours.
- Ask whether the painting has been painted with thick (oil) or thin (water colour) paint.
- Ask which painting they like best. Encourage them to give reasons.
- Suggest that the children make their own picture of the fresh flowers.
- Ask for ideas on how they could make a picture, eg use tissue paper balls, or collage of petal shapes using different fabrics. Encourage ideas using a mixture of media.
- Ask a child to choose a vase and arrange the flowers.

Art activity

- Allow those children who have expressed how they wish to proceed to choose their own materials.

Extension/variation

- Make flowers for the Kwanzaa and The Selfish Giant projects.

Links to home

- Ask parents to allow their child to dismantle a flower to explore its structure.

Related activities

- Paper-making (see pages 24–25)
- Kwanzaa project (see pages 109–112)
- The Selfish Giant project (see pages 145–150)

Resources

- Paintings: *Flowers in a Vase* by Rachel Ruysch (1664–1750); *Hebridean Roses, Eigg* by Winifred Nicholson (1893–1981); *Vase of Flowers* by Odilon Redon (1840–1916); *Flowers in Glass Vase* by Ambrosius Bosschaert (1573–1621); *Sunflowers* by Vincent van Gogh (1853–1890)
- Fresh spring wild flowers
- A choice of vases
- Paints
- Paintbrushes
- Thick paper for base
- Coloured tissue and crêpe papers
- Junk materials
- Coloured pipe cleaners
- Cardboard egg boxes
- Glue and glue spreaders
- Scissors

 Supervise the use of scissors.

Autumn leaves

Media and Materials

• • • • • • • • •

Resources

- Collection of different coloured leaves
- Painting: *Autumn Leaves* by John Everett Millais (1829–1896)
- White paper
- Brown, red, green and orange paper
- Stiff painting brushes
- Toothbrushes
- Small sponges
- Selection of thick paints including brown, orange, green and red
- Trays for paint
- Plastic aprons
- Newspaper
- Cereal box card
- Scissors
- Songs: 'Let Us Dance' and 'Conker, Conker', from *Start with a Song* by Mavis de Mierre (Brilliant Publications)

• • • • • • • • •

 Supervise the use of scissors.

Learning objective

- To explore autumn leaves and make prints

Preparation

- Prior to the activity, the children should have visited a park with a variety of trees to collect autumn leaves.

What to do

Circle time

- Share the children's experiences of the visit to the park.
- Examine the collected leaves. Talk about the texture, colour, number of leaflets (ash leaf, chestnut leaf), the shape of the edges.
- Encourage children to sort and match the leaves.
- Show the painting *Autumn Leaves*. Ask what the children in the picture are doing.

Art activity

- Encourage the children to choose their own colours.
- Support different techniques to make leaf prints:
  - ◆ Spread paint on the leaf and make a print by pressing it on to a sheet of paper.
  - ◆ Place the leaf on clean paper and splatter or dab paint round the edge.
  - ◆ Draw round a leaf on to card. Cut out the inside of the shape to make a stencil. Use different techniques to fill the space, eg splattering paint using different colours. Point out the colours and textures created when different colours are mixed.

Extension/variation

Music activity

- Sing the songs about autumn trees.

Related activities

- Fruitful (see page 26)
- Trees (see page 93)
- The Selfish Giant project (see pages 145–150)

⑥

Tiles

Learning objective
6
- To experiment and make patterned slab tiles

Preparation
- Prepare cardboard templates.
- Wedge the clay to remove air.

What to do
Craft activity
- Encourage the children to roll out a square of clay about 1.5cm thick. Support trimming it to size, using the template.
- Ask them to make shapes, patterns and textures on the surface of the tile by pressing shapes into the surface, engraving or adding material to make a raised shape. If bits of clay are added as decoration they should be joined using 'slip' (clay mixed with water to a liquid consistency).
- The clay can be kept moist by keeping it covered with damp cloths and wrapping it in polythene.
- Ask the children to describe the shapes and patterns they have made. Support language development: *shape*, *pattern*, *decoration*, *triangular*, *rectangular*, *circular*.
- After the clay has hardened, let the children paint the tiles to accentuate the shapes.

- When the clay is 'leather hard', the surface can be painted with different coloured clay 'slips' and then fired in a kiln.
- If the clay tile is not going to be fired, it can be decorated with paint mixed with PVA glue.
- Instead of using clay use playdough.
- Shapes can be cut from thick cardboard, then glued on top of the template.
- Apply white poster paint as a base, then paint.
- On completion, the tiles should be treated with a coat of diluted PVA to make them water-resistant.

Extension/variation
- Mount the tiles together to make a group mural. Discuss how the blocks could be arranged to emphasize the effects of shape, pattern and decoration.

Related activities
- Coloured shapes (see page 20)
- Bricks (see page 30)

Media and Materials

• • • • • • • • • •

Resources
- Cardboard template 7cm x 7cm (for size of tile)
- Clay, modelling clay (see page 172 for suppliers) or playdough (see page 29)
- Knife
- Kiln if required
- Rolling pins
- Tools to model material
- Wooden base board to stick tiles on
- Strong adhesive (for use by practitioner)
- Poster paints
- Paintbrushes
- PVA glue
- Newspaper
- White lining paper
- Thick cardboard

• • • • • • • • • •

 Supervise the use of sharp tools.

Toy soldiers

Media and Materials

Resources
- Cardboard roll from kitchen towel
- Red, blue, black, silver paper
- Glue and spreader
- Black crayon
- Scissors
- Music: *The Parade of the Wooden Toy Soldiers* by Léon Jessel (1871–1942)
- CD player

Supervise the use of scissors.

Learning objective
- To make a paper toy soldier

What to do
Craft activity
- Cut legs at the bottom of the cardboard roll. Wrap round the blue paper to make trousers.

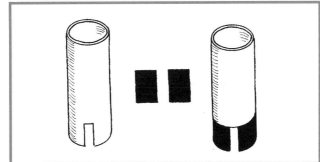

- Wrap red paper round the body and glue into position.
- Roll two tubes of red paper to make arms. Cut one as shown to make a bent arm.

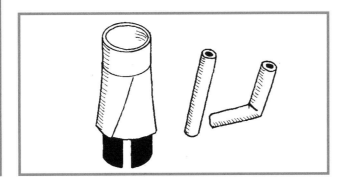

- Glue the arms to the body
- Draw on the eyes and mouth.
- Roll a strip of silver paper to make a gun and glue.
- To make a busby hat, cut out fringing from black paper as shown. Overlap two pieces and stick to the top of the head.

(6)

Extension/variation
Music activity
- Play *The Parade of the Wooden Toy Soldiers*. Ask the children to march their soldiers to the music.

Related activities
- Nutcracker project (see pages 155–159)

Lines

Media and Materials

• • • • • • • • • •

Resources

- Paintings: *Untitled #10* by Agnes Martin (b. 1912); *½ x Series (Blue)* by Robert Mangold (b. 1937); *Onement III* by Barnett Newman (1905–1970)
- Paints
- Paintbrushes
- Trays for mixing colours
- Paper
- Straight-edged objects, eg rulers
- Pencils
- Coloured construction bricks and base

6

Learning objectives
- To construct or paint straight lines
- To notice and comment on patterns

Notes for practitioner
- *Untitled #10* is composed of a repeating pattern of straight thick grey and medium thickness white lines divided by a thin graphite line.
- *½ x Series (Blue)* is made up of panels, the shadows creating straight lines, as well as diagonal pencil lines.
- *Onement III* shows a vertical straight red line through the middle of a maroon background.

What to do

Circle time
- Ask where the children have seen straight (parallel) lines, eg railway lines, on the middle of the road, zigzag lines on the road by school, edges of the pavement, parking restrictions, etc.
- Show painting(s) and ask if they can see any patterns.

Art activity
- Suggest they make pictures to show straight lines.
- Encourage the children to mix colours to show contrasts between the lines.

Extension/variation
- Build constructions with coloured bricks to show straight lines.

Links to home
- Ask parents to point out straight and parallel lines in the environment.

Related activities
- Coloured shapes (see page 20)
- Bricks (see page 30)
- Crossing the road (see page 92)
- Mkeka tablemat (see page 109)

© Mavis Brown
www.brilliantpublications.co.uk

Add water

Media and Materials

• • • • • • • • • •

Resources
- Painting: *Saf Gimmel* by Morris Louis (1912–1962) or similar
- Plain white kitchen towels
- Masking tape
- Thin paints in primary colours (red, yellow, blue)
- Paintbrushes
- Easels
- Sponges
- Water in plastic pot
- Blackcurrant or other concentrated fruit drink
- Clear plastic beakers
- Drinking water
- Coloured felt-tip pens

• • • • • • • • • •

 Note any child with diabetes or allergies to E numbers.

Learning objectives
- To begin to differentiate colours
- To explore colour mixing and dilution

Preparation
- Try the Extension activity first to ensure that your felt-tip pen colour is a mixture of two or more different colours.

Notes for practitioner
- Paintings by Morris Louis such as *Saf Gimmel* are created by running diluted colour down the canvas.

What to do
Circle time
- Show the children the painting. Discuss how it could have been created.

Snack time
- Pour some concentrated fruit drink into a clear plastic beaker. Ask for predictions of what will happen when you add water.
- Support language development: *dilute, concentrated, strong, weak.*
- See what happens; taste what happens.

Art activity
- Fasten a piece of kitchen towel to the sloping easel with masking tape.
- Show the children how to make a wet painting. Paint diluted paint along the top of the kitchen towel and let it drip down the paper.

(8)

- Add water by squeezing the sponge.
- Encourage experimentation with thicker colour and varying the amount of water.
- Let different colours drip on to each other and mix together. Discuss the colours.
- Dry and mount the pictures.

Extension/variation
- Mark a piece of kitchen towel with felt-tip pens. Drip water on to the colour, and let it run. The water will separate the mixture of colours in the felt pen.

Related activities
- Food and shopping topic

Storm

Learning objective
● To paint a storm, using finger painting

What to do
Circle time
● Read *Chimp and Zee and the Big Storm*
● Show the paintings and ask how the children can tell the pictures show a storm.
● Talk about :
   ◆ the composition (in *Pont Neuf in Paris* the horses' manes and woman's cloak and scarf are flying; the woman grips her hat)
   ◆ clouds and colours used (*Sea and Light Clouds* uses stormy colours and a lot of movement in the sky and sea)
   ◆ the texture of the paint (in *Starry Night* or *Road with Cypress and Star* the paints are thick and have been vigorously painted).

Art activity
● For finger painting, support spreading the paint on a plastic surface. A plastic-topped table is ideal.
● The children can comb through the paint to make waves.
● Support making a monotype by laying paper on top of the paint. Press over gently at first, then try further prints by pressing harder.

● Show how mixing with black or white alters the tone of the colour.
● Encourage experimentation to get different textures, eg using a toothbrush to splatter paint.
● Play 'Fingal's Cave' while painting.

Extension/variation
● Paint or make a collage of a large wave on cardboard for the Seaside project.

Links to home
● Ask for old combs.

Related activities
● Seaside project (see pages 160–163)
● Seasons topic
● Water topic

Media and Materials

· · · · · · · · · ·

Resources
■ Book: *Chimp and Zee and the Big Storm* by Catherine and Laurence Anholt (Frances Lincoln)
■ Thick paints: blue, dark green, white, black
■ Spoons
■ Combs
■ Toothbrushes
■ Sponges
■ Printing roller
■ White lining paper
■ Pale blue sugar paper
■ Paintings: *Pont Neuf in Paris* by Louis Anquetin (1861–1932); *Sea and Light Clouds* by Emil Nolde (1867–1957); *Starry Night* or *Road with Cypress and Star* by Vincent van Gogh (1853–1890)
■ Music: Overture from *The Hebrides* 'Fingal's Cave' by Felix Mendelssohn (1809–1847)
■ Glue and spreaders
■ Cardboard boxes
■ Collage materials
■ CD player

© Mavis Brown
www.brilliantpublications.co.uk

Quiet as a mouse

Music and Dance

• • • • • • • • • •

Resources
- Nursery rhyme/song: 'Three Blind Mice'
- Range of percussion instruments, enough for one each
- Song: 'Mouse', from *Start with a Song* by Mavis de Mierre (Brilliant Publications)

Learning objectives
- To show an interest in the way musical instruments sound and to tap out simple repeated rhythms
- To join in favourite songs

What to do
Music activity
- Show each type of instrument and ask what kind of sound it could make.
- Ask if the children can be as 'quiet as a mouse'. See if the class can hand out the instruments without making any sound.
- Allow the children to examine the percussion instruments and find out what sound they do make.
- Sing 'Three Blind Mice' and get the children to clap to the beat (pulse) of four.
- See if the children can add a percussion accompaniment only on the first beat, then be silent for the other three. The children can whisper 'two, three, four'.

Extension/variation
- Learn the song 'Mouse'.

Related activities
- Tick tock (see page 58)
- Rats (see page 105)

Class

Noah's music

Learning objective
- To create movement in response to music

What to do

Circle time
- Read a story about Noah and his ark.
- Talk to the children about how the animals went into the ark, two by two. Discuss how the animals may have arrived at the ark. Compare how the children arrive at the setting, and then walk into the room after break time.
- Go through the different animals represented in *Carnival of Animals* and ask how the animals would move as they make their way to the ark.

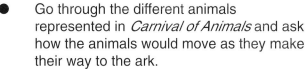

Dance activity
- Play *Carnival of Animals* and ask the children if they can work out which bit of music describes the elephant, the lion, the tortoise. How do they know?
- Ask, 'How are the animals moving?' Ask the children to move like each of the animals.

Extensions/variations
- Ask how shoals of fish move. Choose three leaders for the children to follow. Point out that they need to be aware of the other children around them, and not to bump into each other. Play 'Aquarium' and ask the children to move to the music.
- Encourage the groups to move in the space individually and as a team imaginatively, eg moving across the room in an 'S' shape while swaying their bodies.

Related activities
- Noah's animals (see page 15)
- Bird masks (see page 16)
- Rats (see page 105)

Resources
- Book: Any Noah story such as *Professor Noah's Spaceship* by Brian Wildsmith (Oxford University Press)
- Music: *Carnival of Animals suite* by Camille Saint-Saëns (1835–1921)
  Select:
  1 Royal March of the Lion
  2 Hens and Cocks
  4 Tortoises
  5 The Elephant
  6 Kangaroos
  7 Aquarium
  8 Rabbits and Hares
  19 Aviary
  23 Finale
- CD player

Music and Dance

. . . .

Resources
- Choral and orchestra music: *African Sanctus* by David Fanshawe (b.1942)
- Percussion instruments
- Song: 'I Went to Visit a Farm One Day', from *This Little Puffin* compiled by Elizabeth Matterson (Puffin)
- CD player

Learning objectives
- To sing to themselves and make up simple songs with animals sounds and humming
- To accompany the songs with percussion instruments

Preparation
- Find 'Chants' (Track 10) on the CD, Masai Milking Song (Kenya, 1972) and Turkana Cattle Song (Northern Kenya, 1970).

What to do
Music activity
- Explain to the children that the women believe that if they do not sing to the cows, then the cows may not give them enough milk.
- Play the music and ask whether the men sound like cattle lowing.
- Ask how many different instruments can they hear, (horns, tin whistle, drums, bells).
- Talk with the children about their pets. Encourage them to make up a song to sing to their pet. It does not have to rhyme or even have words.

Extensions/variations
- Encourage the children to make up an accompaniment to their song with a percussion instrument of their choice.
- Sing 'I Went to Visit a Farm One Day'.

Related activities
- Tra-la (see page 65)
- Kwanzaa project (see pages 109–112)

Peter and the Wolf

Learning objectives
● To show an interest in the way musical instruments sound
● To use their imagination in dance and match movements to the music

Preparation
● Make cards showing pictures of each of the characters in *Peter and the Wolf*.

What to do

Circle time
● Show the video that has humans and puppets acting in a humorous way.
● Ask the children why different instruments are used to represent the characters. Discuss the different quality of sounds (*timbre*).
● Support language development for words describing the sounds, such as *trilling*, *dark and sinister*, *cheerful*.
● Talk about each character and how the sounds of the instruments reflect their personality. Show pictures of the instruments.

Dance activity
● Discuss how each character will move to the music.
● As the children practise the movements, call out questions such as: How long or short are their movements? What body shapes are made? How is the character feeling?

● Play the CD that tells the story along with the music.
● Let the children dance each character as it is heard in the music. Hold up the flash cards to support the children.

Extension/variation
● Choose children to play a part for a performance.
● Play the 'Musical Families' game to learn about musical instruments.

Links to home
● Invite parents to a performance.

Related activities
● Noah's animals (see page 15)
● Bird masks (see page 16)

Resources
■ Video: *A Prokofiev Fantasy* with 'Peter and the Wolf' narrated by Sting (Deutsche Grammophon)
■ Television and video recorder
■ Book: *Eyewitness Guides: Music* (Dorling Kindersley) for musical instruments
■ Music: *Peter and the Wolf* by Sergei Prokofiev (1891–1953)
■ CD player
■ Card game: 'Musical Families' (Child's Play)
■ Characters from Peter and the Wolf on cards

Rockin' robin

Music and Dance

• • • • • • • • • •

Resources
- Song: 'Rockin' Robin' by J. Thomas, sung by Jackson 5 or Bobby Day. For the words search 'rokin robin' in the internet
- CD player
- Bird masks (see page 16)
- Bird wings and tails made from brown paper
- Red jumpers/T shirts
- Brown or black or pink stockings

Learning objective
- To dance to a song

Preparation
- This activity is best done during the Christmas period.
- Make bird masks, wings and tails.

What to do
Music activity
- Play the record and discuss making up a dance to the music.
- Ask the children to clap to the beat, then sway to the beat.
- Teach the chorus and when to sing 'Tweet'.
- Go through each verse and ask for suggestions on what movements they should make to the music.
- Draw a line on the floor for the children to stand on.
- Ask the children to do their own dance to the music on the spot as if they are robins perched on a branch.
- Give them time to practise.

Extension/variation
Performance
- Dress up as robins and dance!

Links to home
- Ask to borrow clothes to make up costumes.
- Invite parents to attend the performance.

Related activities
- Noah's animals (see page 15)
- Bird masks (see page 16)
- Stuck up the chimney (see page 76)

⑧

Hip hip hooray

Learning objective

- To recognize repeated sounds and sound patterns

What to do

Circle time

- Show the class the painting *Hip Hip Hooray* of bright figures and animals.
- Ask the children what they think of the painting; what kind of mood does it convey?
- Tell them the title. Ask what they do when they are happy.
- Look at the book *If You're Happy and You Know It.*

Music activity

- Sing 'If You're Happy and You Know It (Clap Your Hands)' with the actions.
- Ask on what other occasions people clap their hands.
- Ask the children to clap as giving applause.
- Tell them that you are going to clap to the rhythm of the words of the song, that is, one clap for each word, or each part of a word (syllable), and include the rests. Clap as you sing.

Extensions/variations

- Clap different rhythms and ask the children to copy.

- Ask the children to clap a short four-beat rhythm over and over again. This is an *ostinato*.

Related activities

- In the mood (see page 55)
- Here comes the bride (see page 118)
- A day to remember (see page 120)

Resources

- Painting: *Hip Hip Hooray* by Karel Appel (b.1921)
- Song: 'If You're Happy and You Know It (Clap Your Hands)', from *This Little Puffin* compiled by Elizabeth Matterson (Puffin)
- Book: *If You're Happy and You Know It* illustrated by Annie Kubler (Child's Play)

Hot cross buns

Music and Dance

• • • • • • • • • •

Resources

■ Flip chart and pen
■ Xylophone, piano or electronic keyboard
■ Song: 'Hot Cross Buns', from *This Little Puffin* compiled by Elizabeth Matterson (Puffin)
■ Book: *Start with a Song* by Mavis de Mierre (Brilliant Publications) for reference

Learning objectives

● To realize that pitch can be notated on paper
● To play by ear

What to do

Music activity

● Learn the song 'Hot Cross Buns'. Talk about high and low notes. Can the children sing a high note? A low note? An even lower note?
● Ask if the second note 'cross' is higher or lower than the first note 'hot'. Sing the note, do not play at this stage. Mark the notes on the board.
● Ask if the third note 'buns' is higher or lower than the notes for 'hot' and 'cross'. Mark the note on the board.
● Explain how musicians write notes on lines, to make it 'easier' to read. Draw a stave (five lines) on the board. (See *This Little Puffin* for the music.)
● Ask the children to play the three notes on an instrument. (Start at middle C, the second note is the C an octave lower, then an E.)
● Give the children time to work out the notes on the instrument while looking at the music.

Extension/variation

Book corner

● Let the children look through books showing music.

Related activities

● Food and shopping topic
● Plant pots (see page 54)
● Bedtime (see page 56)
● Growing plants (see page 94)

Blue boy

Learning objective
- To respond to a picture with sound

What to do
Circle time
- Show the painting *The Blue Boy.*
- Ask the children to describe the colours and the texture of the boy's clothes. (Blue and silky smooth jacket, cloak and breeches. Soft and fluffy feather on the black hat.)
- Ask what they notice about the background. (Obscure trees and cloudy sky to make the portrait stand out.)
- Ask about the expression on the boy's face. Does he look happy, sad, contented, confident? Do they think the boy is rich or poor?

Music activity
- Ask the children which instruments could match how the portrait looks – blue, soft and silky. Can they give their reasons?
- Would the sound be loud or quiet, high or low, slow or fast?
- Let the children try the suggested instruments, and discuss whether their ideas were suitable.

- Ask if there could be a way of playing the instrument to improve the sound, eg instead of hitting a cymbal with the usual beater, could they use something softer?
- Ask what voice sounds could be used.
- Remind the children that silence is also effective.
- Ask them to play two instruments at the same time.
- If using pitched instruments, suggest they try two notes at the same time (chord), eg two notes next to each other, one note interval, etc.
- Record the children's final composition.

Extension/variation
- Play a suitable track from an Evelyn Glennie album, illustrating the use of percussion instruments to convey mood.

Related activities
- Portraits (see page 21)
- Myself (see page 31)

Resources
- Painting: *The Blue Boy* by Thomas Gainsborough (1727–1788)
- Internet: www.huntington.org/ ArtDiv/ BlueBoyPict.html
- Instruments
- Any Evelyn Glennie drumming CD
- CD player
- Tape recorder
- Blank cassette tape

Music and Dance

• • • • • • • • • •

Resources
- Book: *My Dad* by Anthony Browne (Transworld Publishers Ltd)
- Song: 'Oh My Beloved Father', from *Gianni Schicchi* by Giacomo Puccini (1858–1924)
- Song: 'My Heart Belongs to Daddy' by Cole Porter (1891–1964)
- CD or tape player
- Paper
- Paints
- Paintbrushes

Learning objectives
- To show an interest in the way musical instruments and the voice can sound
- To make comparisons

Preparation
- Edit the songs to make them play for a shorter time.

What to do
Circle time
- Read *My Dad*.
- Ask the children if the dad in the story is funny or serious.

Music activity
- Tell the children that they are going to hear some songs about daddies/fathers.
- Ask which song they prefer and to give reasons.
- Explain that a singer with a high-pitched voice is called a soprano.

Extensions/variations
- Ask the children ask for a sentence about a dad. Write the sentences down with the name of the child.
- The children could make a painting of their dad. These could be displayed with their sentences, if appropriate. Alternatively, make a group display.

Links to home
- Check on home relationships before doing this activity.

Related activities
- Grandad's visit (see page 80)
- Hello Grandma (see page 81)

Family fingers

Learning objectives
- To play finger games and join in with singing
- To sing to themselves and make up simple songs

What to do
Circle time
- Read *Toby's Doll's House* and talk about the titles of relatives (uncle, aunt, etc) and who's who.

Music time
- Learn some finger play games and songs.
- Make up a finger play song based upon a family, eg starting at the thumb:

> *Here comes Mum on her way*
> *Here comes Dad lots to say*
> *Here comes Brother very tall*
> *Here comes Sister not so small*
> *Here comes Baby...*(children add their own words)

> *Here comes Grandma fat and jolly*
> *Here comes Grandad driving a lorry*
> *Here comes Uncle very smart*
> *Here comes Auntie with home-made tart*
> *Here comes Cousin...*(children add their own words)

Extension/variation
- Encourage the children to role play and sing using finger puppets.

Links to home
- Ask parents to talk about who's who among their relatives.

Related activities
- Ring around (see page 64)
- Baby games (see page 138)

Music and Dance
• • • • • • • • • •

Resources
- Book: *Toby's Doll's House* by Raynhild Scamell and Adrian Reynolds (David & Charles Children's Books)
- Song: 'Tommy Thumb', from *This Little Puffin* compiled by Elizabeth Matterson (Puffin)
- Book: *Clap Your Hands Finger Rhymes* compiled by Sarah Hayes (Walker Books)
- Finger puppets (see EDUZONE, page 172)

Alternative books
- *First Verses: Finger Rhymes* edited by John Foster (OUP) (also a cassette)
- *Finger Fun and Action Rhymes: Big Book* by Wendy Body (Longman)

Rattle those pans

Music and Dance

Resources
- Video: *STOMP Out Loud* (VCI)
- Television and video recorder
- Bubble wrap
- Cutlery
- Wood blocks
- Different sized tins
- Cardboard boxes
- Pipes
- Car wheel hubs
- Plastic and metal buckets
- Metal dustbins and lids
- Brooms and brushes
- Saucepans
- Frying pans
- String
- Drum
- Small balls of paper

Learning objectives
- To show an interest in the way sounds can be created
- To make up some simple repeated rhythms

Preparation
- Watch video for ideas. The performers use everyday things to make music to which to dance.

What to do
Circle time
- If appropriate, watch *STOMP Out Loud*.
- Discuss the video. Support language development: *vibrate*, *timbre*. Introduce words describing the qualities of sounds, such as *rattling*, *smooth*, *tinkling,* and words relating to sound production, such as *hitting*, *shaking*, *scraping*.

Collection table activity
- Encourage the children to experiment and explore the sounds that are made by everyday items by hitting with a variety of different materials, shaking, blowing on the items.
- Put balls of paper on to a drum. Watch the paper jump as you tap the drum. Tell children they do not need to hit things very hard or rapidly – encourage them to allow items to vibrate.

Extension/variation
- Encourage the children to make up their own rhythms.

Links to home
- Warn parents that children will want to hit different materials in the home, and to guide them to try appropriate items.
- Ask children to find objects that make particular sounds, eg high tinkling sounds, and bring them into school. These could be grouped on the collection table with the describing words written above the objects.

Related activities
- Hum and click (see page 59)
- The park in the dark (see page 66)
- Bobbing boats (see page 70)
- Pop (see page 152)
- Splish drip splosh (see page 165)

Sing a song of soap

(8)

Learning objective
- To sing to themselves and make up simple songs to a beat with words

Preparation
- Make a list of items you can buy that rhyme, eg:
  - ◆ Boiled beef and lettuce leaf
  - ◆ Sherbet pips and crinkly chips
  - ◆ Sudsy soap and fluffy coat

What to do
Circle time
- Read *Teddybears Go Shopping*.
- Support language development of names of shops: *grocery*, *greengrocery*, *bakery*, *chemist*, *supermarket*, *butcher* (or section of supermarket).
- Support language development of what the shops sell.
- Robert Teddybear suggests that the shopping list sounds like a song. Ask why he thinks this. (It rhymes and has a rhythm.)
- Ask the children to make up a song with pairs of rhyming products, like the Teddybears' song, during the session (while they are doing other tasks).
- Suggest using the dictionaries.

- Suggest that the children ask you to write down any ideas they have during the session on to the flip chart.
- Share the ideas at the end of the session.

Extension/variation
- Ask children to decide how the song should be sung, which instruments should accompany it and how they should be played.

Links to home
- Ask that parents play rhyming games with their child.

Resources
- Book: *Teddybears Go Shopping* by Susanna Gretz (A & C Black)
- Flip chart
- Felt-tip pen
- Picture dictionaries
- Percussion instruments

Gardening songs

Music and Dance

• • • • • • • • • •

Resources

- Songs: 'In the Garden and in the Countryside' chapter, including 'I went to the garden' by EMM from *This Little Puffin* compiled by Elizabeth Matterson (Puffin)

Learning objective
- To begin to build a repertoire of songs with actions

What to do
Music activity
- Encourage the children to learn the songs by heart.
- Say the words of each line, and ask the children to repeat them, speaking the words clearly.
- Introduce the melody. Help children who find it difficult to sing in tune by placing them beside the stronger singers.
- Ask the children to hum the starting note of a song before they begin to match the pitch.
- Begin to learn a new song, then go on to a well-known song within a single session.

Extension/variation
- Give children the chance to sing alone. Initially all responses should be accepted and praised.

Related activities
- What has eaten the lettuce? (see page 79)
- A lady scarecrow (see page 114)
- Creepy crawlies project (see pages 125–128)

Class

Plant pots

Learning objective
- To recognize and explore how sounds can be changed by making a pitched instrument from plant pots

Preparation
- Screw cup hooks, well spaced out, into the 4cm side of the length of wood.
- Tie a large knot at one end of the rope and thread through the hole of a plant pot. Tie a loop at the other end of the rope.
- Set up at least three different sized plant pot bells.

What to do

Circle time
- Read one of the books about gardening.
- Suggest finding out whether an instrument could be made from plant pots.

Music activity
- Secure the length of wood between two chairs and suspend the plant pots, like bells, from the hooks. Make it easy to rearrange the pots.
- Ask the children to arrange the pots with the deepest (lowest) pitch on their left and highest notes to the right.
- Ask the children whether they notice anything as regards the size of the pot and the pitch. (The smallest pot will have the highest pitch.)

Extension/variation
- Suggest that the children make up a tune with their pots.

Links to home
- Warn parents that children will want to hit different materials in the home, and to guide them to try appropriate items.

Related activities
- Hot cross buns (see page 47)
- Bedtime (see page 56)
- Growing plants (see page 94)
- I don't believe you (see page 111)

Resources
- Books: *Jasper's Beanstalk* by Nick Butterworth and Mick Inkpen (Hodder Children's Books) or *Jody's Beans* by Malachy Doyle (Walker)
- Clay plant pots of different sizes
- Rhythm sticks or wooden spoons
- Rope (to pass through hole of pots)
- Wood 2.5cm x 4cm x 150cm long
- Cup hooks
- Two chairs

⚠️ Do not let the children hit the pots so hard as to break them or knock them off the hooks.

Music and Dance

• • • • • • • • • •

Resources
- **Jolly song**: 'In the Mood' played by Glenn Miller (trombone), compiled by Garland (Album: 'Glenn Miller Orchestra Essential Jazz') (Sony)
- **Sad song**: 'Ev'ry Time We Say Goodbye' played by Benny Goodman (clarinet), compiled by Cole Porter (Album: 'Benny Goodman and His Great Vocalists') (Legacy)
- **Happy song**: 'On the Sunny Side of the Street' played by Louis Armstrong (trumpet), compiled by Fields, McHugh
- Soft cuddly toys
- Book: *I Love to Cuddle* by Carl Norac (Macdonald Young Books)
- CD player

Learning objective
- To listen to jazz music and show an interest in the way musical instruments sound

What to do
Circle time
- Ask the children what they do when they feel sad.
- Read *I Love to Cuddle* while the children cuddle their toy.
- Ask to see a sad face then a happy face.

Music activity
- Play the recorded songs.
- Explain that the style of music is called jazz and the soloists are playing instruments that you blow – ie a brass instrument (trumpet, trombone) or woodwind (clarinet, saxophone).
- Ask which song is happy and which is sad, and which song/instrument they prefer.

Links to home
- Bring a cuddly toy to the setting (with name label).

Related activity
- Hip hip hooray (see page 46)

Bedtime

Music and Dance

• • • • • • • • • •

Learning objective
● To explore and learn how the pitch of sounds can be changed

What to do

Circle time
● Read one of the poems or rhymes about bedtime and getting up.

Music activity
● Stand the xylophone on its end with longer (low-pitched) notes at the bottom.
● Ask the children to make a high-pitched sound like mice squeaking at the top of the stairs. Play the high notes on the xylophone.
● Ask for a low-pitched note like growling lions at the bottom of the stairs. Play the low notes on the xylophone.
● Ask the children what they notice about the size of the xylophone bars and the pitch of the note. (Longer bars, lower pitch.)
● Hand out the percussion instruments. Let the children experiment to determine the pitch.
● Tell the children that when you play a high note, the children with highpitched instruments (eg the bells and triangles) should respond. Similarly, when you play the low notes, the children with low-pitched instruments (eg the drums) should respond.

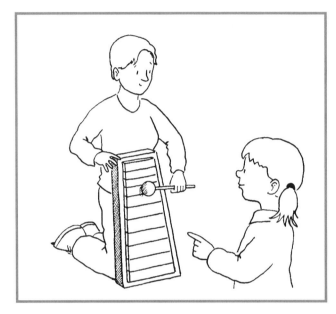

Extensions/variations
● Play 'Going to bed, getting up'. The children describe climbing up the stairs by making their voices rise in pitch, and fall when going downstairs. Sing to the notes of a scale: eg *C D E F G.*
● Tell the children to lie down, close their eyes and listen to *Clair de Lune.* Ask them what pictures the music puts into their mind.

Related activities
● Hot cross buns (see page 47)
● Plant pots (see page 54)
● Growing plants (see page 94)

Resources
■ Poem: 'Ned' by Eleanor Farjeon, from *The Oxford Treasury of Children's Poems* (Oxford University Press)
■ Rhymes: 'Diddle, Diddle Dumpling, My Son John'; 'Through the Day'; 'There Were Ten in the Bed', from *This Little Puffin* compiled by Elizabeth Matterson (Puffin)
■ Poem: 'Get Up' by Michael Rosen, from *Michael Rosen's Book of Nonsense* (Hodder and Stoughton)
■ Wooden xylophone
■ High-pitched percussion instruments such as bells and triangles
■ Low-pitched percussion instrument such as drums
■ Music: *Clair de Lune* by Claude Debussy (1862–1918)
■ CD player

Music and Dance

• • • • • • • • • •

Resources
- Book: *Rosie's Room* by Mandy and Ness (Milet Publishing Ltd)
- Small plastic mirrors
- Large plastic mirror
- Music: 'Andante Second Movement', from *Violin Concerto No. 1 in A Minor* by Johann Sebastian Bach (1685–1750)
- CD player

Learning objective
● To match movements to each other and to music

What to do

Circle time
● Read *Rosie's Room*.
● Let the children experiment with making faces and actions using mirrors.
● Point out how their movements are opposite (when they move their right arm, their reflection shows the left arm moving).

Dance activity
● Remind them of their reflections.
● Sit the children opposite each other in pairs. (It helps if one of the pair is more able. Ask one of them to be leader and make some movements.) Their partner should match the movements as though they are the first child's reflection.
● Swap roles and repeat.
● Repeat the exercise but moving around in the space.
● Suggest holding one hand.
● Suggest facing each other and putting the palm of their hands together.

Extension/variation
● Play slow music (see Resources), and encourage the children to listen first, then modify their sequence of movements to fit to the music.

Tick tock

Music and Dance

• • • • • • • • • •

Learning objective
● To tap out simple repeated rhythms

What to do

Circle time
● Read *Clocks and More Clocks*. Ask why it appeared that the clocks gave the wrong time.
● Show children examples of clocks from the collection table.
● Show the pendulum clock (or a picture of one). Demonstrate with string and bob how a pendulum can swing steadily. Count the swings with the class: 1, 2.
● Shorten the string to make the beat go faster, and ask everyone to count again. Ask if the beats are faster or slower.

Music activity
● Sing 'My Grandfather's Clock' using the metronome if available. Explain it helps everyone to keep to the same beat.

Extension/variation
● Play the two wood blocks as tick-tock as the children sing.

Related activity
● Trains (see page 69)

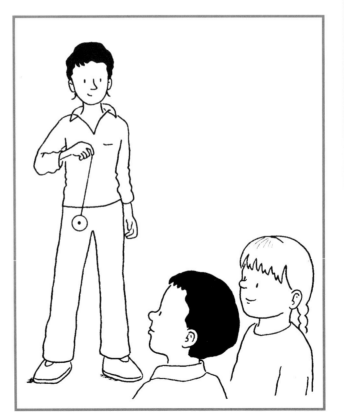

Resources
■ Book: *Clocks and More Clocks* by Pat Hutchins (Bodley Head Children's Books)
■ Collection table with a variety of clocks, including one with a loud tick and a pendulum clock
■ Long pendulum of string with bob at end
■ Song: 'The Clock', from *Start with a Song* by Mavis de Mierre (Brilliant Publications)
■ Song: 'My Grandfather's Clock', see www.kididdles.com
■ Metronome
■ Two wood blocks of different size with beater

Hum and click

Music and Dance

• • • • • • • • • •

Resources
- Poem: 'Bleep' by Michael Rosen, from *Michael Rosen's Book of Nonsense* (Hodder and Stoughton Children's Division)
- Percussion instruments

Learning objectives
- To learn about long and short sounds
- To learn to control and play a percussion instrument

What to do
Circle time
- Read the poem.
- Ask the children to suggest sounds they can hear in the home.
- Ask them to think of some sounds that are long, eg spinning washing machine, hum of fridge, a hair dryer, running water in the bath, lawn mower. Make sure they understand the difference between a sound that continues without a break (sustained) and a succession of short sounds that follow on from each other so quickly that they give the impression of one long sound, ie they are the same pitched note.
- Ask the children to make a long sound with their voices.
- Ask for some short sounds, eg tick of a clock (see Tick tock, page 58), beeping of a computer, snipping scissors.

Music activity
- Hand out the instruments and ask the children whether their instrument makes a short or long sound.
- Demonstrate how the head of a beater will bounce off a vibrating surface (eg a drum head) if you use a loose wrist.
- Ask the children to make either a long or short sound, and to say which it is.
- Ask how a sound can be shortened (eg by touching the vibrating surface). Touching a triangle will prevent it from vibrating.

Extensions/variations
- Divide the children into two groups – long and short sounds. Agree on signals for each group to play in turn. Count to four beats, and get those instruments with short duration, eg tone blocks, maracas, to play each beat.
- Continue counting four beats and ask the children playing instruments with a long duration, eg cymbal or triangle, to make their sounds last for a full four beats.

Related activities
- Tick tock (see page 58)
- Outer space (see page 68)

My body

Class

Learning objective
- To explore and learn how sounds can be made by the body

What to do
Music activity
- Encourage the children to find out how many different sounds they can make using hands, feet, mouth and tongue.
- Ask the children to make sounds, saying the vowels (*a, e, i, o, u*), repeating consonants and diphthongs (eg *chch*).
- Can the children make a fast sound, a slow sound; a high sound, a low sound; a quiet sound, a loud sound?
- What sounds can they make when they move different parts of their bodies?

Extensions/variations
- Ask a child to set the tempo with a steady beat making their chosen sound.
- The rest of the class listen for a few beats, then join in (not too loudly) with their own chosen sound.
- Allow different children to take their turn.

Related activity
- Marching soldiers (see page 157)

Resources
- Book for reference: *The I Can't Sing Book* by Jackie Silberg (Brilliant Publications)

Dee daw

Music and Dance

• • • • • • • • • •

Resources

- Book: Any Trumpton firemen story
- Toy police cars, fire engines, ambulances
- Small-world figures
- Playmat of town
- CD: *Sound Effects* (BBC)
- CD player
- Hand-held percussion instruments

Learning objective
- To investigate how sound changes as its source moves

What to do

Circle time
- Read the story and ask how the children would know that a fire engine was coming.
- Ask what other vehicles make the same warning sound.
- Play the sound effects of vehicle sirens and draw their attention to the sound as it changes.

Music activity
- If the setting does not have a long corridor, this activity can be done outside, provided that there is no wind (for the sound to travel in the opposite direction).
- Ask a child to walk away from the group hitting or shaking an instrument. They are to keep the sound at the same volume.
- Ask the rest of the children what they notice about the sound.
- The percussionist then returns, playing as they walk. Ask the children what differences they notice about the sound.
- Repeat using different instruments.

Notes for the practitioner
- As the child walks away, the sound becomes quieter, and also lower in pitch.
- As the child walks towards you the sound becomes louder and higher. (Note, racing cars: *neeeeow!*)
- Sound needs matter (solid, liquid or gas/air) for it to travel through. More particles vibrate as the sound source gets nearer. More vibration results in a higher pitch.

Extensions/variations
- Let the children play with the vehicles on the playmat.
- Support language development: *siren*, names of vehicles and associated officers, and their functions.

Related activities
- Hats (see page 32)
- Who is knocking? project (see pages 141–144)

Class

The four seasons

• • • • • • • • •

Learning objectives

- To recognize how the sounds made on the violin can be used expressively
- To extend their sound vocabulary
- To make comparisons

What to do

Music activity

- Allow the children to examine the violin, and with support explore the sounds that it can make.
- Play *The Four Seasons* without telling the children the title.
- Ask what pictures are made in their head and how they feel.
- Encourage different ideas and point out that different people have different preferences in music (and art).
- Tell the children the title of the music, and ask them to explore how the music describes the seasons. Encourage the children to use the following words and phrases:
  - ◆ **Structure:** beginning, middle, end. (Beginning is faster and exciting to hook your attention.) How do you know that the piece of music has come to the end? (Lower and slower.)
  - ◆ **Dynamics or volume:** How does this change? (Hot 'Summer' conveyed by quiet passage.)

- ◆ **Tempo or speed:** Allegro means fast, largo means slow. (Adds variety and interest.)
- ◆ **Pitch or high/low notes:** Singing birds in 'Spring', low for the storm in 'Summer'.
- ◆ **Timbre or quality of the sound:** Bright and jolly for 'Spring' and the swirling running notes of the violin as the winds of 'Winter'.
- ◆ **Rhythm or long and short notes:** The pizzicato (plucking) to represent raindrops in 'Winter', long notes of the Adagio in 'Autumn' is the sleeping peasant.
- ◆ **Repeated themes:** The hunt in 'Autumn'.

Extensions/variations

- Bring some music that creates different moods to school from home.
- Compare *The Four Seasons* with Beethoven's *Pastoral Symphony, No 6*.

Links to home

- Encourage parents to attend musical concerts with their children.

Related activity

- Fantastic animals (see page 74)

Resources

- Music: *The Four Seasons* by Antonio Vivaldi (1678–1741)
- Violin and bow
- Musician to play the violin – optional
- Music: *The Pastoral Symphony* (No. 6) by Ludwig van Beethoven (1770–1827)
- CD player

© Mavis Brown
www.brilliantpublications.co.uk

Statues

Music and Dance

• • • • • • • • • •

Resources
- Music: any chart dance music
- CD player

Learning objective
● To respond to sound with body movement

What to do
Dance activity
● Play the music and let the children dance to it. When the music stops they must remain still like statues. Those children moving have to sit down and are out.

Extension/variation
● Children have to stay still like a statue while the music is playing, then move about on the spot when the music stops.

Ring around

• • • • • • • • • •

Learning objectives
● To enjoy joining in with dancing and ring games
● To learn a round song

What to do
Music activity
● Learn any of the songs with the actions.
● Encourage cooperative play and turn-taking.
● Encourage the children to play the ring games during play time.

Extension/variation
● Teach a small group how to sing the round 'Row Your Boat'.

Book corner
● Look at the board books illustrating the songs.

Related activities
● Family fingers (see page 50)
● Baby games (see page 138)

Resources
■ Songs: 'Ring-a-Ring-o-Roses', 'Here We Go Round the Mulberry Bush', 'The Farmer's in His Dell', 'There Was a Princess Long Ago', '(Sally) Go Round the Sun', 'Row Your Boat', from *This Little Puffin* compiled by Elizabeth Matterson (Puffin)
■ Books: *Books with Holes* series (Child's Play)

Tra-la

Music and Dance

• • • • • • • • • •

Resources
■ Book: *Winnie-the-Pooh* by A. A. Milne (Methuen Children's Books)

Learning objective
● To sing to themselves and make up simple songs with melody and nonsense words

What to do
Circle time
● Read from Chapter 2 of *Winnie-the-Pooh.* Winnie is doing his 'Stoutness Exercises' and making up a song with invented words. (This is called scat singing and is often used as an accompaniment to a song, eg *doo be wap.*)
● Ask the children to make up their own song during the session.
● At the end of the session ask volunteers to sing their song to the group.
● Discuss the sounds of the nonsense words when praising their efforts.

Extension/variation
● Suggest that the listeners copy the phrases sung.

Related activity
● Sing to your pet (see page 43)

The park in the dark

Learning objective

- To make sound effects to accompany a story

What to do

Music activity

- Read and show *The Park in the Dark.*
- Discuss what kind of sound effects (instruments and voice/body) could be made for each part of the story, eg old creaking swing, tiptoe downstairs, dustbin alley with cat and mice, Little Gee frightened, witches and goblins, howling tree, playground sounds, the train, running, back upstairs to bed. Let the children experiment with the instruments and make any needed.
- Ask for their ideas and organize the children so each child is playing a different part with an instrument. All the children can say 'Whoopee!' and 'Yaiooee!'
- Encourage the children to play the instruments while you read the story.

Extension/variation

- Ask what was 'the thing' in the story (a train). Ask the children if they could suggest something else that would be frightening in the dark. Ask them to make a sound like their frightening thing.

Links to home

- Ask parents to take their child to a playground and a park.
- Ask for volunteers to support a visit to an adventure playground.

Related activities

- Rattle those pans (see page 51)
- Hum and click (see page 59)
- Trains (see page 69)

Resources

- Book: *The Park in the Dark* by Martin Waddell (Walker Books)
- Book: *The Very Noisy Night* by Diana Hendry (Little Tiger Press) – alternative title
- Bought percussion and home-made instruments
- Junk materials

 Check LEA regulations for visits.

Musical toys

Music and Dance

• • • • • • • • •

Resources

■ Music: *Toy Symphony* by Leopold Mozart (1719–1787)
■ CD player
■ Toy trumpets
■ Water-filled bird whistles
■ Toy drums
■ Rattles
■ Cuckoo-sounding pipes

Learning objective

● To recognize repeated sounds and sound patterns

What to do

Music activity

● Play the music, which includes the use of toy instruments.
● Ask the children which toy instruments would make the sounds (see Resources). If these instruments are not available, substitute alternatives and ask the children which instrument could be used instead.

● Let the children experiment with the toy instruments.
● Play the music and let the children join in with the instruments.
● Ask whether the piece gets faster or slower at the end (*tempo*) or louder or quieter (*volume*) at the end.

Related activities

● Nutcracker project (see pages 155–159)

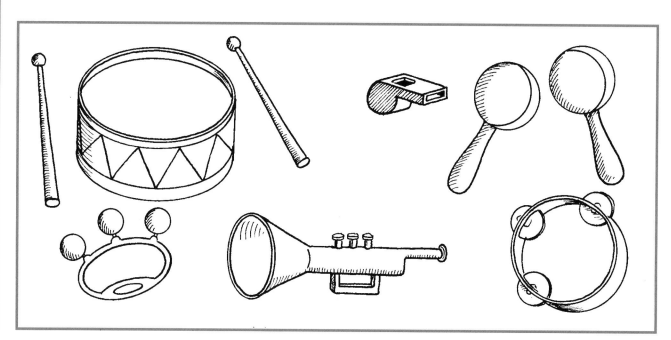

Outer space

Learning objective
- To recognize and explore how sounds can be changed electronically

What to do
Book corner
- Read the poems and encourage the children to join in.

Music activity
- Learn 'Five Little Spacemen' and record one or two children singing it.
- Play back the tape and ask whether they recognize their voice.
- When we hear our own voices we are hearing the sound through the air (which is the same as the sound recorded) and through the head (which is not recorded).
- Ask the children to put their fingers in their ears to hear the sound only through their heads.
- Record two or three different percussion instruments and replay, adjusting the balance and volume. Discuss how different this can make the sounds. Point out that sounds can be changed (electronically).
- Play music by Jean Michel Jarre, who was one of the first musicians to create and play an electronic orchestra.

Notes for practitioner
- MIDI = musical instrument digital interface
- Synthesizer = produces an electronic sound signal sent to the amplifier and loudspeaker.

Extensions/variations
- Explore 'preset' sounds on the electronic keyboard.
- A pair of children can further explore sounds by creating a soundscape describing a spaceship travelling through deep space on the electronic keyboards.
- Play *The Planets Suite* to illustrate how music can be inspired by outer space.

Links to home
- Enquire if any parents can compose with electronic keyboard and effects board. Ask if they would come and demonstrate to the children.

Related activity
- Hum and click (see page 59)

Resources
- Poems: 'Many Ways to Travel' by Tony Mitten and 'Two, One, Zero' by Barbara Ireson, from *Transport Poems* compiled by John Foster (Oxford University Press)
- Song: 'Five Little Spacemen', from *This Little Puffin* compiled by Elizabeth Matterson (Puffin)
- Posters, photographs and nonfiction books of space exploration
- Tape recorder
- Blank cassette tape
- Percussion instruments
- Music: 'The Overture', from *The Essential Jean Michel Jarre* by Jean Michel Jarre (b.1948)
- CD player
- Electronic keyboard with different voices
- Music: *The Planets Suite* by Gustav Holst (1874–1934)
- Internet: search Gustav Holst, select Planets Suite

© Mavis Brown
www.brilliantpublications.co.uk

Trains

Music and Dance

• • • • • • • • • •

Resources

- Music: 'Orient Express', from *The Essential Jean Michel Jarre* by Jean Michel Jarre (b.1948)
- Poem: 'The Train Ride' by June Crebbin, from *The Walker Book of First Rhymes* (Walker Books)
- Pictures of steam, diesel and electric trains
- Instruments
- Song: 'Come to the Station', from *This Little Puffin* compiled by Elizabeth Matterson (Puffin)
- Song: 'The Train', from *Start with a Song* by Mavis de Mierre (Brilliant Publications)
- Music: *Coronation Scott* by Vivian Ellis (1905–1996) (BBC Theme Tunes)
- CD player or tape recorder

Learning objectives

- To show an interest in the way musical instruments sound
- To recognize repeated sounds and sound patterns and tap out simple repeated rhythms

What to do

Music activities

- Play 'Orient Express'. Ask in what ways the music sounds like a train. Explain that the 'clicketty clack' sound of trains was due to the wheels going over the joints in the railway lines.
- Ask the children to experiment with the instruments to find the best one to make the sound of trains.
- Read 'The Train Ride' and accompany the poem with a train rhythm made by the chosen instruments.

Extensions/variations

- Learn one of the songs about trains.
- Play *Coronation Scott* and compare it with 'Orient Express'.

Bobbing boats

• • • • • • • • • •

(8) ## Learning objectives
● To explore the different sounds of instruments and make up simple repeated rhythms
● To begin to build a repertoire of songs

What to do
Music activity
● Show painting *Calm Morning* that shows the artist's children fishing from a boat. Discuss the composition of the picture, pointing out how the artist has highlighted the figures but made the background hazy.
● Learn the song 'Boats', which captures the peaceful setting of the picture.
● Tell the children that when a boat bobs about in the sea, the ropes, metal and wood on the boat slap against each other with the movement.
● Ask the children to experiment and find out what kind of sound is made when these materials hit each other.
● Suggest gentle tapping. Try triangle with metal beater and wooden beater, wood blocks of different pitch, rope against wooden table, etc.

Extensions/variations
● Add the sound accompaniments to the song 'Boats'.
● Learn the words of 'The Sea Is Always Moving'.

Related activities
● Messing about in boats (see page 99)
● Seaside project (see pages 160–163)

Resources
■ Painting: *Calm Morning* by Frank W. Benson (1862–1951)
■ Songs: 'Boats', from *Start with a Song* by Mavis de Mierre (Brilliant Publications) 'The Sea Is Always Moving', from *High Low Dolly Pepper* by Veronica Clark (A & C Black)
■ Percussion instruments
■ Metal, wood objects
■ Skipping ropes

Running water

Music and Dance

• • • • • • • • • •

Resources
- Book: *The Story of Running Water* by Joanna Troughton (Cambridge University Press)
- Nonfiction books about water, rivers, the sea
- Music: 'Winter', from *The Four Seasons* by Antonio Vivaldi (1678–1741); *Arabesque 1* by Claude Debussy (1862–1918); 'Orinoco Flow', from the Watermark album by Enya; The overture from *The Hebrides* 'Fingals Cave' by Felix Mendelssohn (1809–1847)
- CD player
- Sand tray
- Watering cans, sieves, jug, bucket of water

Learning objective
- To begin to move rhythmically

Preparation
- Find the appropriate excerpts on the CDs.

What to do

Circle time
- Read *The Story of Running Water*, which is a folk tale. Ask the children whether it is a true story.
- Tell them that rain falls and runs down the mountain to the rivers, lakes and then to the sea. The water evaporates into clouds. The rain falls from the clouds.
- Support language development: *flow, liquid, sea, river, lake, pond.*
- Illustrate this by using the sand tray – water a mound of sand until water runs from the sand.

Dance activity
- Using the suggested music, tell the story of the rain reaching the sea.
- Encourage the children to dance to each section, imagining that they are the drops of water.

- 'Winter' from *The Four Seasons* sounds like falling rain with 'plop, plop' sounds. Have the children dance separately.
- *Arabesque 1* sounds like running water – down the mountain. The children should begin to move faster and closer to each other into a stream.
- 'Orinoco Flow' sounds like the river 'sailing' into the sea. Encourage the children to move slower and wind around like a meandering river.
- 'Fingals Cave' sounds like a stormy sea. Ask the children to hold hands in groups of four, and imagine that they are waves. Suggest that they run forwards and run backwards or/and lift their arms up and down.

Extension/variation
- Encourage groups of children to make up a sequence of movements to the music.

Links to home
- Invite the parents to a performance.

Related activities
- Splish drip splosh (see page 165)
- Freezing cold project (see pages 168–171)

Today's weather

• • • • • • • • • •

Class

Learning objectives
- To build a repertoire of songs about the weather and sing them from memory
- To explore the different sounds of instruments

Preparation
- The children should know the meaning of the weather symbols.

What to do
Music activity
- Ask the children what the day's weather is.
- Let a child select the appropriate symbol to display.
- On the back of the card list the appropriate songs. Ask the children which song they should sing from the list, eg:
  ◆ Rain: 'In the Puddles'.
  ◆ Cold weather: 'It's a Cold Day' or 'On a Frosty Morning'.
  ◆ Snow: 'Snow Play' and 'Snowflakes'.
  ◆ Wind: 'Wind Song'.
  ◆ Sun: 'Sunshine'.

Extension/variation
- Encourage the children to choose an instrument that makes a sound like the rain or wind, or evokes the feeling of sunshine or cold. Let them demonstrate their chosen instrument to the rest of the group.

Related activities
- Beside the seaside (see page 161)
- Freezing cold project (see page 168–171)

Resources
- Book and CD of songs: *Start with a Song* by Mavis de Mierre (Brilliant Publications)
- Instruments
- Weather symbols on cards

© Mavis Brown
www.brilliantpublications.co.uk

Down at the farm

Imagination

Resources
- Book: *Dora's Eggs* by Julie Sykes (Little Tiger Press)
- Song: 'Old Macdonald Had a Farm', from *This Little Puffin* compiled by Elizabeth Matterson (Puffin)
- Small-world farm
- Small pieces of scrap materials
- Large boxes for animal pens
- Toy farm animals or cardboard models
- Buckets (for feed)
- Large wheeled sit-on toys

 Check LEA regulations for visits. Insist upon hygiene rules – washing hands after handling animals and before eating.

Learning objectives
- To engage in imaginative and role play based on their own first-hand experiences of visiting a farm
- To play alongside other children who are engaged in the same theme

Preparation
- Organize a visit to a small farm that is open to the public. Visit first and check with the LEA its suitability.

What to do
Circle time
- Read *Dora's Eggs* and ask where the farm animals lived.

Music activity
- Sing 'Old Macdonald Had a Farm'.

Small-world activity
- Encourage children to set up a farm with the animals, improvising with scrap materials (eg, corrugated cardboard for ploughed fields, green twisted tissue paper as hedges, blue paper as pond).

Extensions/variations
Outside activity
- Encourage the children to set up a farmyard, using the boxes as sty, hen house, stable and cowshed, and place the animals in the correct place.
- Suggest they ride round the farm to feed the animals (using the buckets).

Links to home
- Ask for volunteers to support a visit to the farm.

Related activities
- Noah's animals (see page 15)
- Sing to your pet (see page 43)

Fantastic animals

Imagination

Learning objective

- To use their imagination in art and design, dance and stories to create a mythological animal

Preparation

- Find section on video and CD/tape.

What to do

Circle time

- Explain that the children are going to see on the video a cartoon of gods and fantastic mythical creatures that the Greeks believed existed many years ago.
  - ◆ Pan plays pipes.
  - ◆ Cupids bring lovers together.
  - ◆ Pegasus is the flying horse.
  - ◆ Centaurs are half human and half horse.
  - ◆ Unicorns are horses with a single horn.
  - ◆ Bacchus is the god of wine and festivals.
  - ◆ Zeus is the King of all the gods.
  - ◆ Hephaestus, his son, makes the thunderbolts.
- (Note: The rainbow has been painted upside-down! The blue colour should be under the curve.)

Story activity

- Ask the children to describe the story. (Pegasus with foals playing, centaurs falling in love and having a party which ends with a thunderstorm. After the storm a rainbow is formed. The sun sets and the moon and stars come out.)

Dance activity

- Play the music. Ask the children to dance, showing how they feel – when the pan pipes are playing (happy), and when the storm comes (frightened).

Extensions/variations

- Ask the children to make a painting, model or collage of a mythological animal of their own.
- Point out that many of the creatures are half animal and half human. Look at the book *Remarkable Animals* and discuss some ideas.

Related activities

- The four seasons (see page 62)
- Monster insects (see page 127)

Resources

- Video: 'The Pastoral Symphony (No. 6)' by Beethoven, in *Fantasia* (Buena Vista–Walt Disney)
- Video recorder and television
- CD or tape player
- Music: *The Pastoral Symphony (No. 6)* by Ludwig van Beethoven (1770–1827)
- Paper, brushes and paints
- Playdough or clay
- Sugar paper or card
- Fabrics, scrap papers, found materials for collage
- Scissors
- PVA glue and spreaders
- Book: *Remarkable Animals* by Tony Meeuwissen (Frances Lincoln)

 Supervise the use of scissors

Teddy's birthday party

Imagination

• • • • • • • • • •

Resources

- Book: *Teddy Bears' Picnic* by Jimmy Kennedy and Prue Theobalds (Uplands Books)
- Resources as requested by the children
- Sand tray and wet sand
- Moulds, bowls and large spoons
- Song: 'Happy Birthday'
- CD-ROM: '2publish', from *Infant Video Toolkit* (2Simple Software)
- Computer and printer
- White card

Learning objective

- To role play a teddy bear's birthday party using available resources

What to do

Circle time

- Read the *Teddy Bears' Picnic*.
- Suggest that the children hold a birthday party, rather than a picnic, for one of the setting's teddy bears. All the toys in the setting can come.
- Ask what items they would need to hold a pretend party in the home corner.

Home corner

- Support the children by helping them to collect resources, as requested.
- Observe the children's use of the resources and their conversation.
- Sing 'Happy Birthday'.

Sand tray

- Suggest making cakes for the party.

Extensions/variations

- Make food from playdough and/or papier-mâché.
- Make a birthday card for Teddy from recycled paper, or use an appropriate computer program.

Related activities

- Paper-making (see pages 24–25)
- Fruitful (see page 26 for papier-mâché)
- Tooth fairy beads (see page 29 for playdough)
- Eat your greens (see page 88)
- A nice cup of tea (see page 101)

8

Stuck up the chimney

Imagination

• • • • • • • • • •

Learning objectives
- To enjoy a song based on Santa Claus and illustrate it with a 3D construction or painting
- To introduce an alternative story line or narrative

What to do
Circle time
- Read the poem *The Night Before Christmas* (first published in 1822).
- Read the words to the song 'When Santa Got Stuck Up the Chimney'. Ask what you would see, if Santa got stuck. Suggest different view points such as seeing him through your window in next door's chimney, or inside your bedroom, etc.
- Ask what might have happened next. The children might suggest soot everywhere, Santa not fitting through the gas fire, etc. Be encouraging to all suggestions.

Art activity
- Suggest making a model of what they would see.
- Support the children when they are working on their model. Encourage them to keep their ideas simple.

Music activity
- Learn the song 'When Santa Got Stuck Up the Chimney'.

Extension/variation
- Paint a picture illustrating the song.

Related activities
- Bricks (see page 30)
- Rockin' robin (see page 45)
- Decorate a tree (see page 86)

Resources
- Book: *The Night Before Christmas* by Clement C. Moore (Walker Books)
- Song: 'When Santa Got Stuck Up the Chimney', from *This Little Puffin* compiled by Elizabeth Matterson (Puffin)
- Paper
- Small boxes
- Cereal card
- Thick blue, black and red paints and paintbrushes
- Cotton wool
- Papier mâché (without fungicide)
- Plasticine
- Pipe cleaners
- Glue and spreaders
- Parcel tape
- Stapler
- Construction bricks and base

• • • • • • • • •

 Supervise the use of the stapler.

Dicing with colour

Imagination

Resources
- Sponge die with colours
- Large flash card with illustrations of movements
- Easel (optional)

Learning objective
- To develop a repertoire of actions by putting a sequence of movements together using colours as the stimulus

Preparation
- Prepare a large sponge die. Stick a different colour to each face, ie white, black, red, green, blue, yellow.
- Make a large card showing the colours matched against simple movements, eg white = arms above the head, black = jump up and down.

What to do
Outside or hall activity
- Explain the game and go over the movements for each colour.
- Display the card so all the children can see it as well as the die.
- Throw the die. Call the colour. The children do the movement.
- Let the children take turns to throw the die.

Extensions/variations
- Let the children choose what movement they will do for each colour. Choose three colours to begin with. First talk about what movements they could do, eg stretch high, crouch low, take little running steps.

- Ask which movements would fit best with each colour, eg red is warm = stretch out, blue is cold = curl into a ball, yellow is sunny = skip.
- Encourage the children to try to link the movements smoothly.

Related activities
- Blue boy (see page 48)
- Musical colours (see page 115)

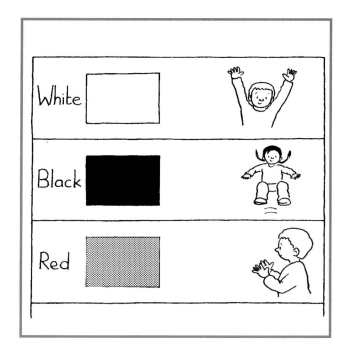

Paint the town red

(8)

Learning objectives
● To differentiate colours
● To paint with plain water outside the setting

What to do

Outside activity
● Tell children that they are going to paint outside to make it look nice.
● Offer them the toy buckets of water. Ask what colour they want to paint.
● Put plastic blocks (or any other items) of that colour into the bucket.
● Hold a conversation with each child about what they are painting on the wall/fence, and what colour they are using.
● Take a photograph of the children and their work.

Extensions/variations
● After a suitable time after the activity go outside.
● Ask what they think has happened to their paintings. Talk about evaporation.

Links to home
● Warn parents that the children will be playing with water, so ask for spare clothes if they need to change.

Related activities
● Homes topic

Resources
■ Clean paintbrushes (to fit in toy buckets)
■ Toy buckets
■ Water
■ Plastic aprons
■ Camera
■ Coloured plastic blocks (or other small coloured items)

What has eaten the lettuce?

Imagination

Resources
- Painting: *L'Escargot* by Henri Matisse (1869–1954)
- Paper
- Paintbrushes
- Paints
- Scissors
- Glue and spreaders
- Glued shapes
- Smooth coloured paper

 Supervise the use of scissors.

Learning objective
- To use their imagination by arranging coloured shapes to represent an object

What to do

Circle time
- Show the painting *L'Escargot (The Snail)* represented by a spiral collage of coloured paper rectangles.
- Ask the children what they think it is. Give them the clue that it will eat the lettuce in their garden.
- Tell them the title. Point out how the rectangles of paper make a spiral shape.
- Suggest that they make a picture from shaped paper.

Art activity
- The children can use cut out or torn coloured paper or handmade paper, or glued paper shapes.
- Ask the children what they are making, and discuss their choice of presentation and use of colours.

Extensions/variations
- Paint paper using mixed colours or print a pattern on the paper first.
- Cut or tear the paper and then use to make the collage.

Related activities
- Coloured shapes (see page 20)
- Paper-making (see pages 24–25)
- Creepy crawlies project (see pages 125–128)
- Gardening topic

Grandad's visit

Class

Learning objectives
● To enjoy stories based on grandparents
● To use their imagination in stories

What to do
Circle time
● Read *Grandfather and I* and ask who has a grandad.
● Ask whose grandfather lives a long way from them, and whether they get to see them.
● Read 'My Grandad in Cyprus', and talk about how they feel when their relatives come to visit them, and what they do.
● Write down their responses, with the child's name next to the contribution.
● Cut out their responses to add them to a display of their paintings.

Extension/variation
Art activity
● Ask the children to paint a picture showing their relatives visiting them.

Links to home
● Find out whether relatives live abroad, so you can prompt the children.

Related activity
● A day to remember (see page 120)

Resources
■ Book: *Grandfather and I* by Helen E. Buckley and Jan Ormerod (Viking)
■ Poem: 'My Grandad in Cyprus' by Michael Xenofontos. from *Poems about Families* selected by A. Earl and D. Senier (Wayland)
■ Flip chart
■ Felt-tip pen
■ Paper
■ Paints
■ Paintbrushes

Hello Grandma

Imagination

Resources
- Book: *The Monster Who Loved Telephones* by John Agard (Longman Book Project)
- Toy telephones

 It is important for children to be able to use a telephone, but warn parents so that they don't run up huge phone bills!

Learning objective
- To notice what adults do, imitating what is observed, and then doing it spontaneously when the adult is not there

What to do

Circle time
- Read *The Monster Who Loved Telephones*.
- Ask why using the telephone makes people happy.
- Ask if they talk to anyone on the telephone.
- Go through how to make a telephone call, but stress that they must have their parents' permission first when using the telephone at home.

Table activity
- In pairs, the children could talk to each other on the toy telephones and pretend that they are talking to a relative such as Grandma.
- Discuss what the children could talk about.

Extension/variation
- Act as a scribe and encourage the children to dictate stories about when their grandma (or other relatives) came to visit.

Links to home
- Ask parents to teach stranger safety, but also to teach their child to know their name, address and telephone number.

Related activity
- A day to remember (see page 120)

Baked beans

● ● ● ● ● ● ● ● ●

Learning objective

6

● To use their imagination in art and stories

What to do

Circle time

● Read the poem 'Beans' about raining baked beans.

● Ask for ideas for anything else that could rain, eg rice pudding. Write the children's ideas down.

Art activity

● Show pictures of pointillist art and discuss whether it looks as though it has rained some kind of food.

● Put the thin sponge into the shallow tray and pour enough thick paint on top so the children can dab their fingers on without dripping. Use a different tray for each colour.

● Encourage the children to finger paint using unmixed colour dabs.

Extensions/variations

Art activity

● Spread glue across the coloured paper.

● Let rice, seeds or pasta drop like rain on to the paper.

● Diluted paint could also be splashed on to the paper and dried food.

Related activity

● Over the rainbow (see page 116)

Resources

■ Poem: 'Beans' by Michael Rosen, from *Michael Rosen's Book of Nonsense* (Hodder and Stoughton Children's Division)

■ Paintings: by Georges Seurat (1859–1891) and Paul Signac (1863–1935)

■ Flip chart

■ Felt-tip pen

■ Thick paint

■ Thin kitchen sponge in tray for paint

■ White lining paper

■ Tables (not easels)

■ Newspapers

■ Plastic aprons

■ Coloured sugar paper

■ Rice, seeds, pasta

■ Glue and spreaders

Shop till you drop

Imagination

Resources

- Book: *Going Shopping* by Sarah Garland (Puffin)
- For home corner, set out like a shop or supermarket: packages and tins with labels, sticky labels for prices, shopping bills, bags
- Cash register and money
- Bar code scanner, eg torch with red light
- Computer
- CD-ROM and playset: *Playskool Store* (Hasbro Interactive)
- Poem: 'More, More, More' by Michael Rosen, from *Michael Rosen's Book of Nonsense* (Hodder and Stoughton Children's Division)

 Don't use plastic bags, to avoid danger of suffocation.

Learning objective

- To role play shopping by pretending that one object represents another, especially when objects have characteristics in common

Preparation

- The children should have visited a shop previous to the activity.

What to do

Circle time

- Read *Going Shopping*. Talk about the names of the shops and what they sell.
- Support language development of names of shops or counters within a supermarket: *grocery, greengrocery, bakery, chemist, supermarket, butcher*.

Home corner

- Ask the children what they need to set out the home corner like a supermarket.
- Support language development.

Book corner

- Read the poem 'More, More, More'.

Extension/variation

Computer activity

- Play with *Playskool Store* (this is a toy till with a scanner and credit card swiper that fits over the computer).

Links to home

- Ask for empty packaging.
- Ask that parents reinforce names for the shops and what they sell.
- Encourage parents to take their child shopping in the supermarket and let them put the food into the shopping trolley.

Related activities

- Sing a song of soap (see page 52)
- Fast food (see page 122)

Soup for sale!

Imagination
• • • • • • • • • •

Learning objectives
(6)
● To play cooperatively as part of a group
● To act out an advertisement for soup

What to do

Role play activity
● Ask the group whether they like soup.
● Ask how the people who make the soup let everyone know about their product (advertising). Ask how and where they can advertise their product. (Posters, adverts in magazines, on the television.) Show the examples that you have.
● Suggest that the group makes a video advert for the soup. Support the children's ideas. (If they say they don't like soup, they could make a video saying how horrible the soup is.)
● Support language development; suggest and encourage adjectives to describe the soup.
● Show the children how to use the camcorder. Let them take turns.
● Discuss the children's plans with them before they start to record the advertisement. Ask how they will set the scene, what props they will need, etc.

Art activity
● Show painting *Soup Can* and talk about how it has been created (printing).
● Ask children to make an advertising poster for their soup. Suggest that they use the computer for their writing.

Extensions/variations

Computer activity
● Show the different labels on the soups. Ask the children to make a label for their own brand of soup.
● Use the computer to do the lettering. You could type in the words, and the children can alter the fonts.

Links to home
● Invite parents to watch the video.
● Ask parents to encourage their child to look at food labels.

Related activities
● Wedding project (see pages 117–120)

Resources
■ Video: television advertisement for soup
■ Advertisement for soup from a magazine
■ Small video camcorder with tape on a tripod
■ Television with video player to play the resulting video
■ Adapter for tape if required
■ Soup tins from different manufacturers with their labels
■ Soup dishes
■ Spoons
■ Tablecloth
■ Painting: *Soup Can* by Andy Warhol (1928–1987)
■ Paper, paints and paintbrushes
■ Computer with different fonts available or CD-ROM: '2publish', from *Infant Video Toolkit* (2Simple Software)
■ Printer and paper

Imagination

Resources

- Book: *Jasper's Beanstalk* by Nick Butterworth and Mick Inkpen (Hodder Children's Books)
- Nonfiction books showing invertebrates
- Magnifying glasses
- Jars for collection of minibeasts
- Plant pots, large stones, logs of wood, compost
- Plants to attract butterflies, eg *Buddlei*
- Small trowels
- Pencils and crayons
- White paper

⚠ Wash hands after working outside. Check children have had a tetanus inoculation.

Learning objectives

- To make habitats for minibeasts
- To make a butterfly garden
- To play alongside other children who are engaged in the same theme

Preparation

- Obtain suitable materials for habitats and plants to attract invertebrates.

What to do

Circle time

- Read *Jasper's Beanstalk*. Talk about the story.
- Talk about where minibeasts can be found (under stones, wood, compost, in water, on plants).

Outside activity

- Take the children out to the garden to look for minibeasts. Ask questions to encourage the children to look closely at the minibeasts, eg How many legs does it have? Does it have wings? Show the children how to use the magnifying glass. (You could use this opportunity to collect a few creatures for closer examination – see Extensions/variations.)
- Suggest that the children make a special home for the minibeasts. How could they arrange the stones etc to make a place the minibeasts would find attractive? Encourage them to work as a group.

- Ask them what they are planning to do.
- Ask them why they are placing the items in their chosen arrangement.
- Make note of imaginative play and conversation.

Extensions/variations

Art activity

- Plan and plant a butterfly garden. Talk about why it is a good idea to put tall plants at the back of a border and small plants at the front. Show the children how to put the plants into the ground.
- Draw the minibeasts then return them to the garden.

Links to home

- Ask parents to look for minibeasts with their child.

Related activities

- Creepy crawlies project (see pages 125–128)

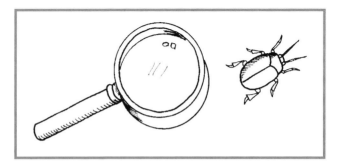

Decorate a tree

Learning objective
- To use their imagination in art

What to do

Art activity
- Suggest to the children that they decorate the twig they have collected or brought from home (see **Links to home**).
- Ask the children what shape their twigs is and what it looks like.
- Encourage the children to add other materials (natural and made) to the twig. Suggest using newspaper rolled in wallpaper paste, fabrics and threads to add texture.
- Add a base to make the decorated twig balance.

Extensions/variations
- Ask the children to describe what they are making and how they are using the materials in their work.
- You could varnish the finished products (away from the children) to make them last longer.
- Decorate a tree in the garden.
- Decorate a tree for Christmas.

Links to home
- Ask parents to help their child obtain an interesting looking twig no more than 50cm long.

Related activities
- Autumn leaves (see page 35)
- Stuck up the chimney (see page 76)
- Trees (see page 93)
- A lady scarecrow (see page 114)

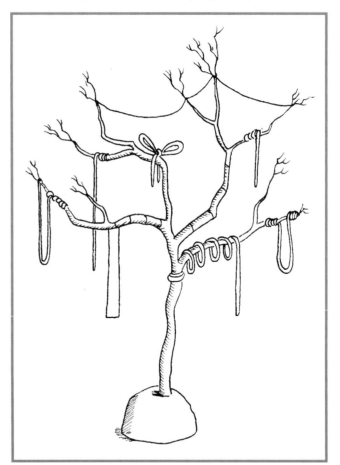

Resources
- Newspaper
- Wallpaper paste (no fungicide)
- Tray for papier-mâché
- Brushes
- PVA glue and spreaders
- Stapler
- String
- Medium sized twigs
- Fabrics and wool
- Material for base (eg Plasticine)
- Varnish (for use by practitioner)
- Christmas tree decorations

Losing a tooth

Imagination

Resources
- Book: *Dave and the Tooth Fairy* by Verna Allette Wilkins (Tamarind Books)
- Book: *How Many Teeth?* by Paul Showers (HarperCollins Children's Books) – alternative title
- White beaded necklace and earrings (see Tooth fairy beads, pages 28–29)

⚠ Closely supervise the children so that they do not play at being a dentist and push something into another child's mouth.

Learning objective
- To enjoy stories based on losing a tooth and to introduce a story line or narrative into their play

What to do
Circle time
- Ask if anyone has been to the dentist. Ask what they should do so they do not get fillings. (Fewer sweets, more crispy fruit, clean teeth, drink milk, and see the dentist.)
- Encourage the children to talk about their own experiences with going to the dentist. Support language development: *tooth*, *teeth*, *dentist*, *decay*, *clean*, *brush*.
- Explain that their teeth fall out when the new (adult) teeth push the baby 'milk' teeth out.
- Read the story *Dave and the Tooth Fairy*.
- Ask the children to use their imagination to decide what the tooth fairy does with all the little children's teeth. (Make jewellery that keeps them invisible?)

Role playing
- Encourage two children to pretend to be tooth fairies admiring their jewellery made from teeth.

Extension/variation
- Eat a piece of apple after or instead of milk at snack time.

Links to home
- Tell parents about the topic. Ask for donations of an apple for snack time.

Related activities
- Tooth fairy beads (see pages 28–29)
- Teddy is ill project (see pages 129–132)

Eat your greens

Learning objective
- To role play, in a group, a dinner table conflict

What to do
Circle time
- Read *Eat Up, Gemma*. Ask the children what they had for dinner the previous day. Talk about likes and dislikes in food. Talk about which foods are good for you, and will keep you healthy, and those foods you should eat in moderation.
- Support language development: names of food, names of courses (*soup*, *main meal*, *pudding* or *dessert*), flavours and appearance.
- Read 'Christine Crump', which describes a girl who eats too many crisps and ends up with indigestion.

Role playing
- Choose who will play the parts of Mum, Dad and two children.
- Get the children to lay the table and pretend to serve dinner.
- One of the children wants to eat only crisps for dinner. The other characters must persuade him/her to eat their greens.
- Encourage the children to collect together the props they need for the role play.

Extension/variation
- Role play the poem.

Links to home
- Warn parents that you will be asking the children what they had for dinner the previous day.

Related activities
- Teddy's birthday party (see page 75)
- A nice cup of tea (see page 101)

Resources
- Book: *Eat Up, Gemma* by Sarah Hayes and Jan Ormerod (Walker Books)
- Home corner with oven, sink, table and chairs
- Plates, cutlery, saucepans, pretend food, spoons, cooking utensils
- Packet of crisps
- Coloured paper
- Poem: 'Christine Crump' by Colin West, from *The Orchard Book of Funny Poems* (Orchard)

© Mavis Brown
www.brilliantpublications.co.uk

My home

Imagination

Resources
- Book: *Toby's Doll's House* by Raynhild Scamell and Adrian Reynolds (David & Charles Children's Books)
- Doll's house and furniture

Learning objective
- To play with the doll's house and compare it with their own home

What to do

Circle time
- Read *Toby's Doll's House*.
- Talk about why the children think that Toby wanted a doll's house for a present, rather any of the other gifts.

Imaginative play activity
- Let the children play with the doll's house.
- Support language development: names of rooms, *bedroom*, *kitchen*, *lounge*, *dining room*.

Extensions/variations
- Ask them to arrange the furniture in the same way that it is arranged in their own home.
- Ask in what way the doll's house is different from their home (other than size).
- Talk about what their home looks like.
- Support language development: *flat*, *bungalow*, *house*.

Related activity
- Bricks (see page 30)

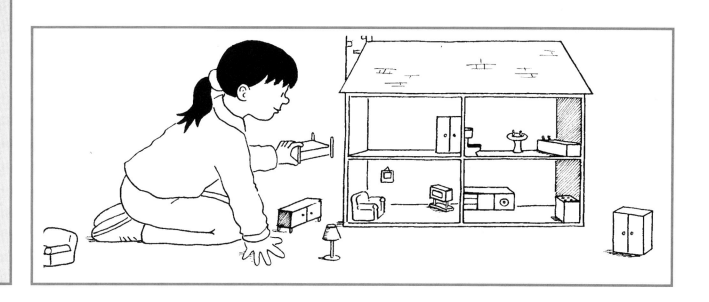

Moving house

Learning objective
(2)
- To engage in imaginative and role play based on their own first-hand experiences

What to do

Circle time
- Read *Moving House*. Ask if anyone remembers moving home. Talk about moving home and what has to be planned.
- Read 'The New Neighbour' and ask who has had a new neighbour.

Role play activity
- Ask what other things the children might ask a child when they meet for the first time.
- In pairs, ask the children to make conversation with each other by asking questions as though they have just moved in next door.
- If the children have not moved house, they could make up what might happen.

Extension/variation
- Practitioner sings the song 'My Old Man Said Follow the Van', and asks the children to listen to the words. Ask what the song is about. (Moving house because they cannot pay the rent.)

Links to home
- Ask parents whether they have moved home recently, so you can prompt the children.

Resources
- Book: *Moving House* by Anne Civardi and Stephen Cartwright (Usborne First Experiences)
- Poem: 'The New Neighbour' by Rose Fyleman, from *Friends Sense and Nonsense Poems for Young Children* compiled by Suzanne and Jane Bottomley (Macdonald)
- Internet: search Marie Lloyd and 'music hall' for words to song: 'My Old Man Said Follow the Van'

Imagination

Resources
- Book: *Cinderella*
- Photographs of (separately) child, their family, and three others, eg their home, pet, garden, car
- Three A4 sheets of paper folded to A5, and stapled to make a book
- White paper
- Computer and printer
- Coloured magazines with pictures of people, homes, gardens, toys, playground equipment, etc, as required
- Scissors
- Crayons
- Glue and spreaders
- Guillotine (for use by practitioner)
- CD-ROM '2publish' from *Infant Video Toolkit* (2Simple Software)

Supervise the use of scissors.

Learning objective
- To use their imagination in art, design and stories

Preparation
- Collect magazines and pictures for activity.
- Prepare booklets.
- Access word processing program on computer, eg '2publish', and select suitable layout for books.

What to do
Circle time
- Read *Cinderella* up to the point where the fairy godmother changes Cinderella for the ball.
- If a fairy godmother could change them, and their homes and gardens etc, how would the children like them to be?
- Suggest that they make a book to show their ideas.

Computer activity
- Support printing text for the booklet.
  - ◆ **Page 1 (title)**
    My life, . . . by
  - ◆ **Pages 2–3**
    This is me . . . but I would like to be like this.
  - ◆ **Pages 4–5**
    This is my home . . . but I would like to live here, etc.
  - ◆ **Page 6**
    This is my family . . . but I love them as they are!

- Add their own drawings to the text.

Art activity
- Stick the collage and photographs on white paper first, then into the booklet when the child is satisfied with their efforts.
- Left-sided page will show their photographs and the right side will be made of a collage from magazines to show their imaginary ideas.
- For example, opposite the photograph of their dog could be a cut-out picture of a dinosaur; opposite their flat could be a picture of a fairy castle, and their garden could be a jungle or pictures of playground equipment on a drawn grass background.

Extensions/variations
- The children could do drawings of themselves, homes, etc instead of using photographs.
- Give the booklet as a Mother's or Father's Day gift.

Links to home
- Ask parents for photographs that can be used.

Related activity
- Over the rainbow (see page 116)

6

Crossing the road

Imagination

. . . .

Learning objective
● To learn to cross the road safely

Preparation
● Draw a road on the playground using chalk. The road should be big enough for use by the outdoor wheeled toys. Include a road crossing.

What to do

Outside activity
● Play at crossing the road. Teach the children the Green Cross Code.
● Support language development: *stop*, *go*, *wait*, *left*, *right*, *cross*.

Imaginative play activity
● Use the playmat and/or construction toys and vehicles to role play crossing the road.

Visit
● Organize a trip out of the setting to use a pelican crossing, and observe the traffic lights.

Music activity
● Learn a road safety song (see Resources).

Extensions/variations
● Ask the school crossing patrol person to come and talk to the children.
● Read 'Lollypop Lady'.

Links to home
● Ask parents to reinforce the use of pelican crossings, and the Green Cross Code.
● Ask volunteers to come and help to practise the Green Cross Code in the playground.
● Ask volunteers to take children to use a pelican crossing.

Related activities
● Hats (see page 32)
● Lines (see page 38)
● Dee daw (see page 61)
● Transport and travel topic

Resources
■ Chalk
■ Outdoor wheeled toys
■ Traffic lights
■ Construction kit to make wheeled vehicles, roadways, traffic lights
■ Playmat with town streets (see Wildgoose products, page 172)
■ Toy vehicles
■ Songs: Safety songs from *This Little Puffin* compiled by Elizabeth Matterson (Puffin)
■ Poem: 'Lollypop Lady' by John Agard, from *The Oxford Treasury of Children's Poems* (Oxford University Press)

. . . .

⚠ Ensure proper adult:child ratio for visit.

© Mavis Brown
www.brilliantpublications.co.uk

Trees

Imagination

Resources
- Nonfiction books or posters showing trees
- Thick paints: green, russet, orange, brown
- White paper
- Thick cardboard
- Black or brown crayons
- Brown fabric or brown wrapping paper
- Brown jumpers/T shirts etc for children
- Glue and glue spreaders
- Newspaper
- Wallpaper paste (no fungicide)
- Scissors
- Elastic bands
- Painting: *Four Trees* by Egon Schiele (1890–1918)

⚠️ A high ratio of helpers to children is required if working near water or in public parks. Take note of any poisonous plants. Care with scissors.

Learning objective
- To use their imagination in art and design when making a tree costume

Preparation
- Check out the park before the visit.

What to do

Circle time
- Talk about the changes in appearance of trees through the seasons.

Visit
- Visit an environment that has different trees.
- Repeat the visit through different seasons.
- Make bark rubbings on brown wrapping paper and with brown crayons.
- Collect fallen leaves and twigs.

Art work
- Look at the painting *Four Trees* and talk about the shape of the trees.
- Working in pairs, make tree costumes, using the bark rubbings for the trunk. Discuss that it has to be easy to put on and take off.
- For ideas for making blossoms and fruit, see pages 145 and 26.

Extension/variation
- Discuss how to attach leaves and blossoms so they can be dropped in the play *The Selfish Giant*.

Links to home
- Ask parents to join the class in a walk round a suitable park or an ecology centre that has trees.

Related activities
- Fruitful (see page 26)
- Autumn leaves (see page 35)
- Decorate a tree (see page 86)
- The Selfish Giant project (see pages 145–150)

Growing plants

Class

Learning objective
- To use their imagination in music and dance

Preparation
- The children should have an understanding of pitch, and the germination of seeds.

What to do
Circle time
- Read *Rachel's Roses* stressing the appearance of the garden through the seasons.
- Talk about how plants grow from seeds. Remind them of earlier work they have done growing seeds and plants.

Dance activity
- Using the xylophone as accompaniment remind children of high pitch and low pitch.
- Hand out percussion instruments and allow the children to remind themselves which instrument is high-or low-pitched.
- Divide the group into two teams – dancers and orchestra (later the children can swap roles and take turns).
- Ask the dancers to imagine that they are seeds that grow into flowering plants.
- Ask the players whether the sounds should be low or high for the root/growing/flowering.

- Support language development: parts of the plant, *root*, *shoot*, *stem*, *leaves*, *flower*.
- Talk the children through the actions.
- As the root emerges from the seed in the ground low notes are played.
- As the plants grow the children play the xylophones, slowly running up the scales.
- As the flowers open, the high notes are played.

Extension/variation
- Conclude the dance with a mime to represent the flower making the fruit that dries, and finally the plant shrivelling and dying.

Related activities
- Hot cross buns (see page 47)
- Plant pots (see page 54)
- Bedtime (see page 56)

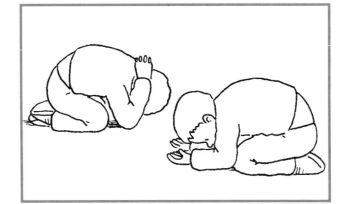

Resources
- Book: *Rachel's Roses* by Karen Christensen (Barefoot Books)
- Pitched instruments such as wooden xylophone
- High-pitched percussion instrument such as bells and triangle
- Low-pitched percussion instrument such as drums

Pebble pet

Imagination

• • • • • • • • • •

Resources
- Smooth hand-sized pebbles
- String
- PVA glue
- Thick paints
- Paintbrushes
- Playdough
- Fabric
- Varnish (for use by practitioner)

Learning objective
- To make a pebble pet and play with it

Preparation
- Collect enough pebbles for the group.

What to do

Art activity
- Make a pebble pet by painting the stone, adding ears and tail with paint, fabric or playdough.
- When the pet is dry, the practitioner can varnish it to stop the paint from rubbing off.

Show and tell activity
- Show the pets, and talk about what they like, what kind of animal they might be, and their name, what they eat, etc.

Extensions/variations
- Encourage two or three children to play with their pebble pets together.
- Talk about how water has worn down stone to make it a pebble.

Links to home
- Ask any parents visiting the seaside to bring back some pebbles.

Related activities
- Seaside project (see pages 160–163)

8

A bear hunt

● ● ● ● ● ● ● ● ● ●

(6)

Learning objective
● To play 'Hunt the Teddy', putting together a sequence of movements

Preparation
● Hide a teddy in a cupboard or other dark place in the setting.

What to do
Circle time
● Read *We're Going on a Bear Hunt* and do the actions.

Imaginative play activity
● Tell the children that they are going on a bear hunt to find Teddy.
● Act out the poem with the children, pretending to travel through the obstacles.

Extension/variation
● Other stuffed animals/toys could be substituted.

Related activities
● Teddy's birthday party (see page 75)
● How will Teddy get there? (see page 98)
● Teddy is ill project (see pages 129–132)
● Goldilocks project (see pages 133–136)

Resources
■ Book: *We're Going on a Bear Hunt* by Michael Rosen and Helen Oxenbury (Walker Books)
■ Teddy bear

www.brilliantpublications.co.uk

Clowns

Imagination

• • • • • • • • • •

Resources
- Video: *Pagliacci* by Ruggero Leoncavallo (1857–1919) (Philips 1982 version with Plácido Domingo, filmed by Franco Zeffirelli)
- Face paints
- Cotton wool
- Towels
- White paper plates and crayons
- Fabrics and wool
- Glue and spreaders
- Camera
- Elastic
- Song: 'Tears of a Clown' by Smokey Robinson
- CD or tape player
- Video recorder and television

Learning objective
- To use their imagination in art and dance

Preparation
- Find Act II, Scene 2, on the *Pagliacci* video.

What to do
Wet playtime activity
- Tell the children that you are going to show them a video of a play about clowns. Act II, Scene 2, contains a slapstick routine.
- Explain that the style of singing is called an opera. Point out that the language is Italian. This is because the composer was Italian. Explain the singers have to be trained.
- Support language development: *soprano* (Nedda) sings very high; *tenor* (Canio) sings high; *baritone* (Tonio) sings low.

Art activity
- Ask the children to paint a face of a clown on a paper plate.
- An adult can then copy the design on the child's face, using face paints.
- Take photographs of the children.

Dance activity
- Play 'Tears of a Clown'. Encourage the children to dance to the music as though they are clowns.

Extensions/variations
- Draw the children's attention to the appearance of the harlequin clown in *The Nutcracker Ballet*. How does his appearance differ from the clowns that you have seen?
- Make the plate into a mask. Cut out eyeholes and attach elastic.

Notes for practitioner
- *Pagliacci* is a story about a clown, Canio, whose beautiful young wife, Nedda, loves a young man, Silvio. Canio sings at the end of Act I 'Vesti la giubba', heartbroken at his wife's infidelity. The drama concludes tragically during the clowns' performance, when jealous Canio stabs his wife and her lover.
- However, this production does show traditional clowns in costume (Harlequin, Columbine and Pagliaccio) with an amusing slapstick routine in Act II, Scene 2.

Link to home
- Check for skin allergies prior to using face paints.

Related activities
- Nutcracker project (see pages 155–159)
- Noah's animals (see page 15) for masks

How will Teddy get there?

Class

Learning objective
● To introduce a story line or narrative into their play

What to do
Circle time
● Learn the words and tune of 'The Bear Went Over the Mountain'.
● Ask the children to suggest alternative ways for the large bear to travel over the mountain, eg *hopped*, *skipped*.
● The song says that the bear saw the other side of the mountain. Ask the children to describe what they think the bear really saw.

Outside or hall activity
● Sit the children in a circle and sing the song.
● Ask the children to remember the alternative words they thought up during circle time. Let the child who suggests a word, eg *hop*, hop with the large teddy bear round the circle, while everyone sings the song.

Extension/variation
Sand tray activity
● Pile up a mound of sand in the sand tray. Provide the children with small plastic bears. Encourage the children to sing the song to themselves as they play.

Related activities
● Teddy's birthday party (see page 75)
● A bear hunt (see page 96)
● Teddy is ill (see pages 129–132)
● Goldilocks project (see pages 133–136)

Resources
■ Large teddy bear
■ Song: 'The Bear Went Over the Mountain', from *This Little Puffin* compiled by Elizabeth Matterson (Puffin)
■ Sand tray
■ Plastic bears

Imagination

Resources

- Poem: 'A Good Play' by R. L. Stevenson from *The Oxford Treasury of Children's Poems* (Oxford University Press)
- Props for making a boat
- Song: 'We Sail the Ocean Blue', from *HMS Pinafore* by W. S. Gilbert (1836–1911) and Arthur Sullivan (1842–1900)
- CD player
- Water tray
- Objects that float, sink
- Small pots and polystyrene trays
- Empty washing-up liquid bottles
- Plasticine

⚠ Supervise the water tray.

Learning objective
- To use available resources to create props to support imaginative play

What to do
Imaginative play activity
- Read the poem 'A Good Play'. Ask the children what they could use to make a pretend boat.
- Support collecting the props, and the children's imaginative play in the boat.
- Play the song 'We Sail the Ocean Blue' as the children play.

Extensions/variations
Water tray activity
- Put objects that float and sink into the water: small pots and polystyrene trays, empty washing-up liquid bottles (a jet of water can to used to push a boat along), Plasticine, etc.
- Support language development: *sink*, *float*, *heavy*, *light*, *sail*.

Related activities
- Bobbing boats (see page 70)
- Seaside project (see pages 160–163)

Are we there yet?

Imagination
• • • • • • • • • •

Learning objective
6
● To engage in imaginative play based on going on a trip

What to do
Circle time
● Read the poems, and ask the children if that is how they felt about going on a trip.
● Encourage the children to talk about their own day out.

Imaginative play activity
● While playing on the mat, encourage the children to pretend that they are going in a car to a theme park or seaside.
● Ask them what they can see on their journey.
● Ask how they feel about going on the trip, and what they might do when they get there.

Music activity
● Learn the song 'Going by Car'.

Extensions/variations
● Read the story *Are We There Yet?*
● The father in this story is in a wheelchair. There could be discussion about equal opportunities and access when disabled people go out. Some of the children may be disabled, others may have disabled parents.

Links to home
● Tell parents about the activity, and ask them to talk to their child about a day out that they have experienced recently.

Related activities
● Seaside project (see pages 160–163)

Resources
■ Poems: 'Are We Nearly There Yet?' and 'I Feel Sick', from *Wish You Were Here (And I Wasn't)* by Colin McNaughton (Walker Books)
■ Wheeled toys
■ Toy cars
■ Playmat of road in the country
■ Song: 'Going by Car', from *Start with a Song* by Mavis de Mierre (Brilliant Publications)
■ Book: *Are We There Yet?* by Verna Allette Wilkins (Tamarind Books)

Imagination

• • • • • • • • • •

Resources
- Book: 'Mad Hatter's Tea Party', from *Alice in Wonderland* by Lewis Carroll
- Song: 'I'm a Little Teapot', from *This Little Puffin* compiled by Elizabeth Matterson (Puffin)
- Soft chairs
- Plates, cups and saucers
- Teapot, milk jug and sugar bowl
- Spoons
- Brown paper cut in squares to look like sliced bread
- Yellow, pink, green, red paper (to make sandwiches)

Learning objectives
- To pretend that one object represents another, especially when objects have characteristics in common
- To notice what adults do, imitating what is observed and then doing it spontaneously when the adult is not there

Preparation
- Set up the home corner as a lounge.

What to do
Circle time
- Read the excerpt 'Mad Hatter's Tea Party' from *Alice in Wonderland*.

Home corner activity
- Ask for a cup of tea, and encourage the children to pretend making a cup of tea.
- Encourage the children to pretend to make and serve sandwiches.

Extension/variation
Music activity
- Learn the action song 'I'm a Little Teapot'.

Links to home
- Suggest to parents that they allow their child to help put out crockery and cutlery on the table.

Related activities
- Teddy's birthday party (see page 75)
- Eat your greens (see page 88)

Under my umbrella

Learning objectives

- To develop a repertoire of actions by putting a sequence of movements together
- To use their imagination in music and dance

Preparation

- If appropriate, find Gene Kelley dancing in the rain on the video.
- Have on view the painting *The Umbrellas*.

What to do

Indoor playtime activity

- Watch *Singing in the Rain* – excerpt of Gene Kelley dancing in the rain. Alternatively, read *Alfie's Feet*.
- Ask whether the children have ever been caught in the rain. Ask if they had an umbrella.
- Ask how it felt. Talk about the differences between warm summer rain and cold winter rain.

Dance activity

- Play 'Raindrops Keep Falling on My Head'.
- Ask the children to pretend it has started to rain and they are putting up their umbrellas, and to skip round the room.
- When the rain stops they close their umbrellas.

Role play activity

- Encourage dressing up and role play the experience of being out in the rain.
- Support language development: *pour*, *drizzle*, *shower*.

Music activity

- Play any of the songs and encourage the children to mime to the music.

Extension/variation

- Learn the words of 'Singing in the Rain'.

Links to home

- Ask to borrow umbrellas for the dance.

Related activities

- Storm (see page 40)
- Running water (see page 71)
- Freezing cold project (see pages 168–171)
- Weather topic

Resources

- Video: *Singing in the Rain* – excerpt of Gene Kelley dancing in the rain
- Video recorder and television
- Painting: *The Umbrellas* Pierre-Auguste Renoir (1841–1919)
- Book: *Alfie's Feet* by Shirley Hughes (Red Fox) – alternative resource
- Umbrellas, raincoats, Wellington boots
- Song: 'Raindrops Keep Falling on My Head' by Burt Bacharach
- CD player
- Songs: 'In the Puddles' and 'Umbrella', from *Start with a Song* by Mavis de Mierre (Brilliant Publications)
- CD and book: 'Singing in the Rain' from *I Can Sing, I Can Colour* (IMP)

What to wear

Imagination

• • • • • • • • • •

Resources
- Children's clothes, gloves, scarves, hats, footwear and accessories for a range of weathers
- Large drawings of weather symbols on card
- Paper
- Crayons
- Computer
- CD-ROM: *Primary Geography: Weather Teddy 1* (Granada Learning)

Learning objectives
- To use available resources to create props
- To support role play based on own first-hand experiences of dressing for the weather

Preparation
- Prepare cards with weather symbols – sun for hot and sunny or summer; cloud and raindrops for wet; snowman for cold or winter.
- Children should have had a previous lesson on the weather and the weather symbols.
- Load CD-ROM into computer and access program.

What to do
Circle time
- Remind children of the weather symbols on the cards.
- Hold up a piece of clothing and ask in what kind of weather you would wear it. What would you wear in hot/cold/wet weather? Why?
- Hold up a floppy hat and ask whether you can wear it in windy weather. Ask for reasons.

Role playing
- Show the children two weather symbol cards, eg wet and hot. Encourage them to choose and dress up in appropriate clothes.

Extension/variation
Computer activity
- Use *Weather Teddy* program to dress Teddy.

Links to home
- Ask for donations of dressing-up clothes.
- Ask parents to encourage their child to choose for themselves appropriate clothes for outdoor activities.

Related activities
- Time to go home (see page 19)
- Storm (see page 40)
- Today's weather (see page 72)
- Seaside project (see pages 160–163)
- Freezing cold project (see pages 168–171)

Windy weather

Imagination

Learning objective
- To use their imagination in music

Preparation
- Prepare a tape of the wind blowing from the sound effects CD.

What to do
Music activity
- Read 'The Wind Came Running'.
- Play the sound effects CD, and ask the children to first think inside their head how to make sounds like the wind with their voices.
- Go round the circle and ask each child to make a sound like the wind with their voice.
- Ask all the children to make their wind sounds very quietly. Put a finger to your mouth to encourage a quiet sound.
- Ask children to make the sound louder, medium volume, then louder still. Signal this by bringing hands away from each other as the sound becomes louder. (Do not raise and lower your hand to signal quiet and loud, as that signal is used to indicate changes in pitch.)
- Support language development: *loud*, *quiet*, *crescendo*, *volume*.

- When the children have learned 'The Wind Finds', divide the group into two.
- One group make the sound effects, and the other sing.
- End with playing the percussion instruments with a bang.

Extensions/variations
- Accompany the poem 'The Wind Came Running' with the children's sound effects, varying the volume.
- Read *Chimp and Zee and the Big Storm*.

Resources
- CD: *BBC Sound Effects* (BBC Worldwide)
- CD player
- Poem: 'The Wind Came Running' by Ivy O. Eastwick, from *Days Like This* compiled by Simon James (Walker Books)
- Song: 'The Wind Finds', from *Start with a Song* by Mavis de Mierre (Brilliant Publications)
- Percussion instruments
- Book: *Chimp and Zee and the Big Storm* by Catherine and Laurence Anholt (Frances Lincoln)

Rats

Communication

(Pied Piper project)

• • • • • • • • • •

Resources

- New Reading 360, Big Book Play: *The Pied Piper of Hamelin* (Ginn and Co)
- Audio cassette: *The Pied Piper of Hamelin and Other Poems:* (Naxos Audiobooks) – alternative resource
- Different textured fabrics
- Fur fabric
- Cereal box card
- Scissors
- Brown or black wool
- Red pom-poms
- Black felt
- PVA glue and spreaders
- Sticky tape
- Black pipe cleaners
- Elastic
- Tape recorder

• • • • • • • • • •

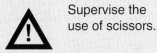
⚠ Supervise the use of scissors.

Learning objective
- To make a rat mask

Preparation
- The children need to have heard the Pied Piper of Hamelin story.

What to do
Craft activity
- Ask the children to describe how the fabrics feel.
- Ask which fabric would make a furry animal like a rat.
- Support cutting out shapes for the face and ears from card and from fabric. Cut out for child's nose.
- Make a cone for nose. Cut as shown, fold the tabs back and stick to face.

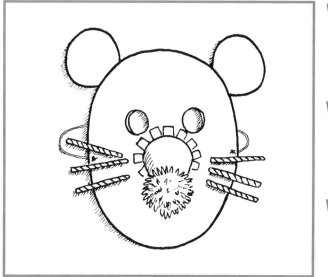

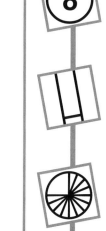

- Stick on ears and glue the fabric on to the cardboard.
- Complete the rat mask with pipe cleaners for whiskers and red pom-pom on the nose.
- Support tying elastic.
- Note the interest shown by the children.

Extension/variation
- Use in the play *The Pied Piper of Hamelin* as rat masks for the children.

Links to home
- Ask for help with the cutting out and sticking.

Related activities
- Nutcracker project (see pages 155–159)

Piping music

Learning objective

- To mime to *The Pied Piper of Hamelin*

Preparation

- Check suitability and prepare music. For ease of organization, the recommended CD has all the required tracks.

What to do

Circle time

- Read *The Pied Piper of Hamelin.*
- Play the music and discuss the way the music represents the characters in the play.

Dance activity

- Play each track and encourage the children to dance, showing the appropriate emotions.
  - ◆ **Scene 1:** Entry of the councillors and Mayor, rats running around, and entry of the Pied Piper – *Concerto No. 2, K314, in D: III–Allegro* by Mozart. The children could play percussion instruments to represent the knock at the door.
  - ◆ **Scene 2:** Rats following Pied Piper and drowning – *Flight of the Bumble Bee* by Rimsky-Korsakov.
  - ◆ **Scene 3:** Townspeople dancing with joy – *Belfast Hornpipe*, traditional.
  - ◆ Argument between Mayor and Pied Piper – *Concerto, Wq 169, in G: III – Presto* by C. P. E. Bach.
  - ◆ **Scene 4:** Children skipping and following Pied Piper – *Sonata, Op. 1 No. 11 in F, IV–Allegro* by Handel.
  - ◆ Lame boy left behind – *Sonata, Op. 1 No. 11 in F, III–Siciliana* by Handel. Children could play percussion instruments to represent the landslide.
  - ◆ **Scene 5:** Townspeople grieving – *Adagio of Spartacus and Phrygia* by Khatchaturian.

Extension/variation

- Combine with other related activities to create a performance.

Links to home

- Ask parents to help with making costumes.
- Invite parents to the performance.

Resources

- New Reading 360, Big Book Play: *The Pied Piper of Hamelin* (Ginn and Co)
- Internet search: Pied Piper of Hamelin
- Music: *James Galway A Portrait*
- CD player
- Percussion instruments

Hamelin

Communication

(Pied Piper project)

• • • • • • • • • •

Resources

■ New Reading 360, Big Book Play: *The Pied Piper of Hamelin* (Ginn and Co)

Learning objective

● To engage in imaginative role play based on *The Pied Piper of Hamelin*

What to do

Circle time

● Read the story with the children.

Role play activity

● What did the rats do to the town? (Ate everything except metal.) Let the children pretend to be rats eating everything.

● How did the councillors and people of Hamelin feel about being invaded by the rats? (Very frightened.) Show me how you would look if you were frightened.

● What ideas did they have to get rid of the rats, and why would they not work? (Lots of cats – but they were dead. Poisoned food – food nearly gone, and poison did not kill them.)

● What did the Piper look like? (Tall with bright clothes and a feather in his cap. He had a gold pipe.)

● How much money did he want to get rid of the rats? (A thousand florins.)

● How much did the Mayor say he would give him? (Fifty thousand florins.) Is this more or less money?

● Did the Pied Piper get rid of the rats? (They followed him as he played and they drowned in the river.)

● How did the people of Hamelin feel? (Very happy.) What would they do to show they were happy? Show me how you would look if you were happy.

● Did the Mayor pay the Piper? (Only offered to pay fifty florins.) Is this more or less than what the Piper asked for? (Much less.)

● What did the Piper do? (Enticed all the children away to a cave. They became trapped inside and were never seen again.) Show me how you would look angry.

● How did the people of Hamelin know what happened to their children? (A boy who could not dance could not keep up and was left behind.) Show me how sad the townspeople would look.

Pied Piper of Hamelin

Class

Learning objectives
● To contribute to the play *The Pied Piper of Hamelin* through a wide range of activities
● To play cooperatively as part of a group to act out a narrative

Preparation
● The children require the experience and attainment of skills provided through the other activities in the project.

What to do
Circle time
● Read *The Pied Piper of Hamelin.*
● Discuss what can be made for the play.
● Choose the actors for the parts.

Dance activity
● Practise the dancing and miming. Support the children by asking how the people and rats would move.
● Encourage them to listen and move to the music.
● Agree upon hand signals to help them relate their movements to the music.

Art activity
● After the mime and dance activity, ask the children to paint a picture or make a collage to illustrate the story.
● Ask them to make a plan of Hamelin and the countryside around the town.

Craft activity
● Make some rat masks (see page 105).
● Make some hats for the councillors, townspeople and the Pied Piper (see pages 32–33).

Extensions/variations
● Involve the whole group in the production.
● Ask which activity they liked best.

Links to home
● Ask for parents to help with costumes.

Resources
■ New Reading 360, Big Book Play: *The Pied Piper of Hamelin* (Ginn and Co)
■ Internet search: Pied Piper of Hamelin
■ Music: *James Galway: A Portrait*
■ CD player
■ See other activities in the project for resources

Mkeka tablemat

Communication

(Kwanzaa project)

• • • • • • • • • •

Resources

■ Woven wool with obvious warp and weft threads
■ Tartan fabric
■ Strips of brown, black, green and red paper or fabric
■ Sugar paper base
■ Glue and spreaders
■ Notched plastic lids
■ Black, green, red wool
■ Scissors
■ Sticky tape
■ Plastic bodkin
■ Sticky-back plastic or laminator

• • • • • • • • • •

⚠ Supervise the use of scissors.

Learning objectives
● To use ideas involving in and out
● To explore colour, texture and space in three dimensions by weaving a tablemat

Preparation
● Make notches in a plastic lid as shown.

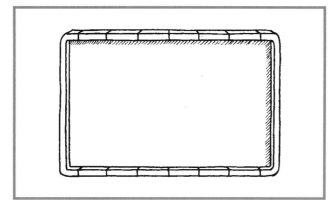

What to do

Circle time
● Show woven materials. Ask the children how the fabric is made.

Craft activity
● Demonstrate weaving on plastic lid with wool.
● Weave using green, black and red wool. Wind sticky tape round the end of the wool to make it stiff, or use a plastic bodkin.
● Alternatively weave using strips of green, black and red paper or fabric to make a large mat.

● Encourage the children to talk about the pattern that they are making.

Extensions/variations
● The straw mat (*Mkeka*) symbolizes tradition in the Kwanzaa celebration. Weave a large brown mat as the centrepiece for the fruit and vegetables. It can be covered with sticky-back plastic or laminated.
● Use the woven material to make a collage or greetings cards.

Links to home
● Ask parents to talk to their child about how clothes can be made by sewing, crochet and knitting.

Related activities
● Paper-making (see pages 24–25)
● Lines (see page 38)

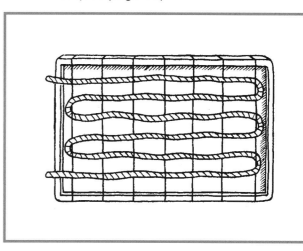

Zulu music

Communication

(Kwanzaa project)

• • • • • • • • • •

Resources

- CD or tape of Zulu warrior dancers and drummers
- Drums of different sizes (large selection in MES catalogue – see page 172)
- CD player

Learning objectives

- To respond to sound with body movement
- To tap out simple repeated rhythms, and make some up

Preparation

- Find a suitable section on the CD/tape to play.

Notes for practitioners

- Creativity (*Kuumba*) is one of the seven basic values of African culture reinforced during Kwanzaa.
- The language used during the festival is Swahili.

What to do

Music activity

- Play the music and ask the children to clap or stamp to the beat. (Zulu music has a strong repeating beat with a solo singer who sings a refrain to which the ensemble replies in harmony.)

Extensions/variations

- Let the children play with drums of different sizes and explore the sounds they make.
- Encourage them to make up their own rhythms.

Related activity

- Sing to your pet (see page 43)

Class

I don't believe you

Communication

(Kwanzaa project)

• • • • • • • • • •

Resources
- Book: *Too Much Talk* by Angela Shelf Medearis (Walker Books) – a West African folktale
- Examples of African art, eg carved statuettes, masks
- African thumb piano (see MES, page 172)

Learning objectives
- To develop a repertoire of actions by putting a sequence of movements together
- To engage in imaginative role play based on own first-hand experiences

Notes for practitioner
- The sixth day of the festival of Kwanzaa celebrates creativity (*Kuumba*).
- The seventh day celebrates faith (*Imani*) and there is a feast (*Karamu*) when the children are given gifts that must include a book and an item representing African heritage, eg a carving.

What to do
Circle time
- Read the story *Too Much Talk*, showing the pictures.
- Ask the children if they have ever had a shock that make them jump. Ask the children to show surprise on their face.
- Can they run fast? Show how you would feel after running uphill and downhill.
- Did the chief in the story believe the farmer, fisherman, weaver and swimmer at first? Have you ever not believed someone? Have you ever not been believed? Show disbelief on your face.
- What made the chief believe them at the end of the story? (The chief's chair spoke.)

Role play activity
- Read the story again, and ask the children to act out the characters' responses, using their face and gestures.
- Play the thumb piano rising in pitch as the children pretend to run uphill, and falling in pitch for running downhill.

Extensions/variations
- Draw attention to the patterns on the costumes and style of illustration in the story book.
- Discuss the African art on the collections table.

Related activities
- Hot cross buns (see page 47)
- Bedtime (see page 56)
- Growing plants (see page 94)

Class

Kwanzaa

Learning objective

- To respond in a variety of ways to what they see, hear, smell, touch and feel while being involved in the celebration of Kwanzaa

Preparation

- Use the internet to obtain more detailed information on this Afro-American cultural holiday created in 1966 by Dr Maulana Karenga. It takes place for seven days from 26th December to 1st January.

What to do

Circle time

- Explain that the principle of the festival is to celebrate the history, values, family, community and culture of the Afro-American (Caribbean) people and of Africans as a whole.
- Encourage the children to dress up in the African costumes.
- On each day greet the children in Swahili: *Habari Gani?*, and teach them to answer with one of the seven principles (*Nguzo Saba*), eg *Umoja* on the first day. (See Kinara for Kwanzaa, page 18.)
- Light one of the candles on the *Kinara*.
- Prepare for the feast (*Karamu*). Involve the children in decorating the setting in the colours of black (unity and pride), red (struggles of the past) and green (hope for the future).

- Explain simply the symbolism of the seven items as they are placed on the mat (*Mkeka*); with the candle holder (*Kinara*) and the seven candles (*Mishumaa Saba*):
  - the cup of unity (*Kikombe cha umoja*), the unity of the family, the community, African nation and race;
  - gifts (*Zawadi*), the love and commitment between parents and children;
  - the harvest fruits and vegetables (*Mazao*), the rewards of labour;
  - an ear of sweet corn (*Muhindi*) for each child, the nation's future.
- Add the African artwork to the display.

Extensions/variations

- The display can be laid upon the green, red and black flag (*Bendera*) in front of the poster listing the seven principles (see internet site).
- Invite a visitor to lead the Kwanzaa feast.

Links to home

- Invite parents to join in with the celebrations.

Related activities

- Kinara for Kwanzaa (see page 18)
- Fruitful (see page 26)
- Atishoo (see page 27) for tablecloth or gift
- Tooth fairy beads (see page 28) for gift
- Sing to your pet (see page 43)

Communication

(Kwanzaa project)

• • • • • • • • • •

Resources

- Internet: www.officialkwanzaa website.org
- candleholder (*Kinara*) and 3 red, 1 black, 3 green candles
- Ears of sweetcorn
- African fruit and vegetables, real or made by children
- Food to share
- Large cup
- Small wrapped gifts
- Woven mats (*Mkeka*)
- Books showing African life, folktales
- Examples of African art, eg statuettes
- Decorations coloured red, black and green
- African music and musical instruments
- CD player
- African costumes for dressing-up

• • • • • • • • • •

 Care with candles and matches.

Make a rainbow

Communication

(Over the rainbow project)

• • • • • • • • • •

Resources

- Painting: *The Blind Girl* by Sir John Everett Millais (1829–1896), shows double rainbow, thunder clouds
- Painting: *The Rainbow* by Georges Seurat (1859–1891)
- Clear plastic tank with water
- Mirror to fit into tank
- A sunny day
- Coloured paper
- Colour magazines
- Glue with spreaders
- Scissors
- Paints
- Brushes, sponges
- Blue paper as background
- Coloured cellophane
- Playdough

• • • • • • • • • •

Supervise the use of scissors.

Learning objectives

- To differentiate colours
- To show an interest in how a rainbow can be made

Preparation

- Set up the mirror in the plastic tank with water, as shown in the diagram.

What to do

Circle time

Make a rainbow

- Let the sun shine through the water in the box.
- Tilt the mirror inside the box so the sun hits the mirror and reflects on to the ceiling.

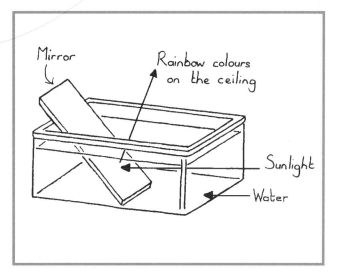

Mirror

Rainbow colours on the ceiling

Sunlight

Water

- Ask the children what they notice about the rainbow. What are the colours?
- Show the paintings and discuss the composition and use of colour.

Art activity

- Suggest that the children make a rainbow.
- Ask what shape it should be.
- Ask what colours, and in what order.
- Ask what materials they are going to use. Supply a variety of materials, but let the children choose.

Notes for practitioner

- A rainbow is part of a circle but we only see half of it. The red is always at the top of the curve and blue is under the curve. To see a rainbow the sun has to be low in the sky (early morning or evening). The sunlight is bent by the raindrops and is split into the separate colours.

Extension/variation

- Talk to the children about how their intentions have been realized.

Links to home

- Ask parents to encourage their child to name the colours that they see.

(4)

A lady scarecrow

Learning objective
● To make a colourful scarecrow puppet

Preparation
● Load the CD-ROM.

What to do

Circle time
● Show the video of *The Wizard of Oz*.
● Suggest that the scarecrow would be happier if he had a friend.

Craft activity
● Make the body from stuffed stockings.
● Fasten a cane along the back so it can be stuck into the ground.
● Dress the puppet in colourful fabric.
● Talk to the children about the texture of the fabrics and their colour.

Extensions/variations
● The children can make a tin man and/or lion puppet.
● The scarecrow can be a gift and put in a window box.
● Play the CD-ROM *OZ-Interactive Storybook*.

Related activities
● Gardening topic

Communication
(Over the rainbow project)

● ● ● ● ● ● ● ● ● ●

Resources
■ Video: *The Wizard of Oz* directed by Victor Fleming (1939) (MGM)
■ Story: *The Wonderful Wizard of Oz* by L. Frank Baum (optional)
■ Internet: search Wizard of Oz
■ Junk material, fabric, wool
■ Nylon stockings
■ Material for stuffing
■ PVA glue and spreaders
■ Scissors
■ Garden canes
■ String
■ Cardboard tubes
■ Boxes
■ Aluminium foil
■ CD-ROM *OZ-Interactive Storybook* (Dorling Kindersley)
■ Computer
■ Video recorder and television

● ● ● ● ● ● ● ● ● ●

 Supervise the use of garden canes and scissors.

Communication

(Over the rainbow project)

• • • • • • • • • •

Resources
- Music: *Clair de Lune* by Claude Debussy (1862–1918)
- CD player
- Scarves (cut up voile curtains) in the colours of the rainbow or streamers (see MES, page 172)

Learning objectives
- To explore space and create movement in response to music
- To move rhythmically, representing a rainbow

What to do
Dance activity
- Lie down on the floor and listen to the piano music.
- Ask the children to imagine themselves dancing to the music.
- Ask them what kind of steps they will take. (Fast, but close together.)
- Ask how they would move around the room. (Suggest they weave around and rise and fall in the vertical plane.)
- Tell them to get up and dance to the music.
- Make sure they have enough room around them and give them a scarf each. Ask them to practise wafting the scarf up and down.

- Divide the group into two, and ask each group in turn to run with their little steps and waft the scarves behind them.
- Ask them to describe what the dance looks like.

Extensions/variations
- Suggest that each child is part of a rainbow. Ask them to organize themselves into the correct colour sequence.
- Talk about the shape of a rainbow and the order of the colours.
- Discuss how to make up a dance with the music to represent a rainbow.

Related activity
- Dicing with colour (see page 77)

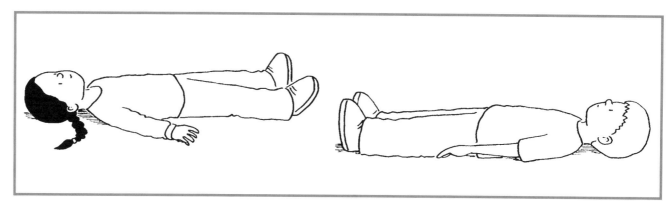

Over the rainbow

(8)

Learning objectives
● To use their imagination in art
● To express and communicate their ideas using paint

Preparation
● Find some examples of paintings by Georges Seurat or Paul Signac. They painted in a style called pointillism, with lots of little dots of colour instead of brush strokes.

What to do
Circle time
● Play the song 'Somewhere Over the Rainbow'.
● Suggest to the children that there is a magical place over the rainbow where the colours are different.
● Show painting *Pine in St Tropez* by Signac. (He favoured pink, blue, orange, purple, red and green spots.)

Art activity
● Let the children choose a photograph from which to get ideas.
● Suggest that the children use small pieces of potato to print to get a similar effect. Put fat kitchen sponges in shallow trays and pour thick ready-mixed paint on top to make paint pads. Use one tray for each colour.
● Talk to the children about the magical place over the rainbow.

Extension/variation
● Children paint a composition with coloured spots.

Related activity
● My imaginary life (see page 91)

Resources
■ Song: 'Somewhere Over the Rainbow' sung by Judy Garland, from *The Wizard of Oz* (film, 1939)
■ CD and book: 'Somewhere Over the Rainbow', from *I Can Sing, I Can Colour* (IMP, see page 172)
■ Internet: search Wizard of Oz
■ Clear simple photographs from magazines of houses, animals, etc
■ Paintings by Georges Seurat (1859–1891) and Paul Signac
■ Painting: *Pine in St Tropez* by Paul Signac (1863–1935)
■ Thick ready-mixed paints
■ Thin flat kitchen sponges
■ Shallow trays
■ Pieces of potato that can be gripped by child
■ Newspaper
■ Plastic aprons
■ CD player

© Mavis Brown
www.brilliantpublications.co.uk

Communication

(Wedding project)

• • • • • • • • • •

Resources

- Book: *When Willy Went to the Wedding* by Judith Kerr (Picture Lions)
- Wedding photograph
- 2 pieces thick white card 50mm longer and wider than the photograph
- Stiff cardboard same size to use as backing for frame
- White card
- Pencils, rulers
- Cutting board
- Scissors and craft knife
- Guillotine for practitioner's use
- PVA glue and spreaders
- Different shapes of pasta or shells
- Varnish (for use by practitioner)

• • • • • • • • • •

 Use shells if allergic to wheat. Supervise the use of cutting tools.

Learning objective

- To use ideas involving fitting, overlapping and enclosure when making a photograph frame

Preparation

- A photograph taken during the role play wedding (see page 120) can be used.

What to do

Circle time

- Read *When Willy Went to the Wedding.*
- Discuss how people can keep memories of an event by taking photographs.

Craft activity

- Support placing the photograph in the centre of one of the pieces of card and drawing round the photograph with a pencil and ruler.
- Support cutting out the centre.
- Place the different pasta shapes on to this card. Support language development: *repeating pattern, sequence, arrangement.*
- Try not to leave any gaps.
- When satisfied with the arrangement, glue the pasta to the card.
- Glue the photograph on to the second card.
- Leave to dry overnight. An adult could varnish the pasta.
- Cut into the second piece of cardboard as shown and fold on the dotted line to make a stand.
- Glue the three pieces of card together.
- Question the children about their frame.

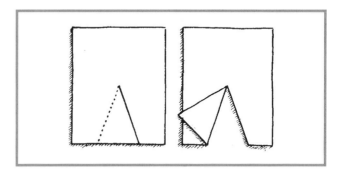

Related activity

- Portraits (see page 21)

② (2)

Here comes the bride

Learning objectives

● To begin to build a repertoire of songs
● To communicate thoughts and feelings through a variety of songs

What to do

Circle time

● Play *Wedding March* ('Here Comes the Bride').
● Explain that the bride and groom can choose hymns, music and poems for their wedding ceremony.

Music activity

● Play the songs 'Magic Moments' and 'Congratulations'.
● Ask when the songs should be played – at the beginning or end of the ceremony?
● Let the children choose two hymns for the wedding ceremony, then teach them to the group so they can sing them from memory.

Extensions/variations

● Read *Who Do You Love?* or/and *Guess How Much I Love You.*
● Encourage the children to think up some poems for a wedding.

Links to home

● Ask parents to talk to their child about the parents' or relatives' wedding if appropriate.

Resources

■ Book: *Who Do You Love?* by Martin Waddell (Walker Books)
■ Book: Guess *How Much I Love You* by Sam McBratney (Walker Books)
■ Music: *Wedding March* by Felix Mendelssohn (1809–1847)
■ Song: 'Magic Moments' sung by Perry Como, by Burt Bacharach
■ Song: 'Congratulations' sung by Cliff Richard
■ CD Player
■ Piano
■ Children's hymn book

© Mavis Brown
www.brilliantpublications.co.uk

Wedding cake

Communication

(Wedding project)

• • • • • • • • • •

Resources

■ Book: *Maisie Middleton at the Wedding* by Nita Sowter (Picture Lions)
■ Book: *When Willy Went to the Wedding* by Judith Kerr (Picture Lions) – alternative title
■ Photographs of wedding cakes
■ Cardboard boxes of reducing sizes
■ Different papers – tissue, metallic
■ Small artificial flowers
■ Papier-mâché (no fungicide in the paste)
■ White lining paper
■ Scissors
■ Glue and spreaders
■ Paper and pencils or crayons
■ Pipe cleaners
■ Self-hardening clay
■ Paints
■ Paintbrushes

• • • • • • • • • •

 Supervise the use of scissors.

Learning objectives

● To use ideas involving fitting and overlapping by making a model wedding cake
● To talk about personal intentions, describing what they were trying to do
● To respond to comments and questions, entering into dialogue about their creations

What to do

Circle time

● Read one of the stories. Ask what kind of food they have at a wedding. Ask if anyone can describe a wedding cake. Show photographs.

Craft activity

● Make a three-tier wedding cake using cardboard boxes. Encourage the children to work collaboratively.
● Ask about their design, giving support on techniques.
● Decorate each box using different materials. Rolled and twisted paper can form relief designs.
● Discuss durability and balance of the decorations on the model. Are the decorations stuck on well?
● Ask whether the three tiers will balance. Discuss choice of materials and their properties.

Extensions/variations

● Make a different shaped cake.
● Make a bride and groom to fit on top.

Links to home

● Ask parents for photographs of wedding cakes (label photographs with name).

Related activity

● Paper-making (see pages 24–25)

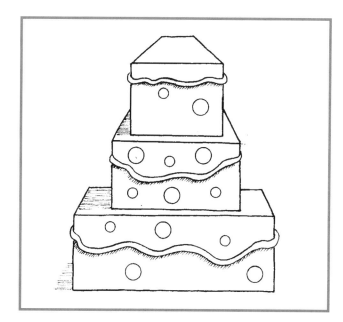

A day to remember

Learning objective
- To role play a Christian wedding based on their own first-hand experiences

Preparation
- Check photographs and videos.
- Simplify the wedding vows.

What to do
Circle time
- Show photographs of children as bridesmaids/pageboys. Ask if anyone has attended a wedding. Ask about their experiences. Talk about the significance of the occasion. Ask about special clothes, special food, presents given and why.
- Read the story *Maisie Middleton at the Wedding*. Talk about the problems of wearing bridesmaid's dresses.
- Allow the children to talk about anything funny that happened at the wedding they attended.
- Show short clips from videos of weddings.

Role play activity
- Discuss who attends a wedding and who the key people are. Support language development: *bride, groom, vicar, priest, registrar, bridesmaids, pageboys, parents, witnesses.*

- Involve the whole class in dressing up and re-enacting a wedding.
- Play the music.
- Record the role play with photographs and video. Allow children to take photographs.

Extension/variation
- Invite someone to come in and talk about a non-Christian wedding.

Links to home
- Ask for wedding photographs showing their child as a bridesmaid/pageboy.
- Ask parents to talk to their child about the parents' or relatives' wedding if appropriate.
- Ask to borrow bridesmaid's dresses, white dresses for use as a bride's dress. Ask for parents' help in making any accessories.
- Invite parents to watch wedding role play.

Related activities
- Mehendi hand (see page 17)
- Portraits (see page 21)
- Hats (see page 32)
- Spring flowers (see page 34)
- Soup for sale! (see page 84) for using camcorder
- Toast (see page 121) for food
- Blossom (see page 145) for confetti

Resources
- Book: *Maisie Middleton at the Wedding* by Nita Sowter (Picture Lions)
- Book: *When Willy Went to the Wedding* by Judith Kerr (Picture Lions) – alternative title
- Dressing-up clothes suitable for wedding role play
- Artificial flowers and cake (see Related activities)
- Wedding photographs, videos
- Video player and television
- Music: *Wedding March* by Felix Mendelssohn (1809–1847)
- Chosen hymns
- Camcorder and camera

© Mavis Brown
www.brilliantpublications.co.uk

Toast

Communication

(King's breakfast project)

• • • • • • • • • •

Resources

- Poem: *The King's Breakfast* by A. A. Milne (Egmont Children's Books)
- Poem: 'Slice, Slice, the Bread Looks Nice', from *This Little Puffin* compiled by Elizabeth Matterson (Puffin)
- Toaster
- Plates
- Knives for spreading
- Margarine
- Choice of spreads, eg yeast spread, jam, etc
- Knife for cutting
- Bread board
- Brown playdough
- Rolling pins and tools to mark playdough
- Knife
- Paints and paintbrushes

• • • • • • • • • •

> ⚠ Wash hands before doing the activity. Keep toaster away from children. Care with knives. Do not include peanut butter.

Learning objective
- To explore colour, texture, shape, form and space in three dimensions by making sculptures based upon toast

What to do

Circle time
- Read *The King's Breakfast*.
- Support language development: Alderney is a breed of cow (similar to a Jersey); a dairymaid's job is to milk the cow; names of spreads.

Snack time
- Support making toast and spreading margarine and choice of spreads, eg yeast spread, jam, honey, marmalade.
- Point out the textures and colours of the toast and spreads.
- Encourage good manners at the table.
- As a group recite 'Slice, Slice, the Bread Looks Nice'. Alter the words to include whatever spread(s) you are using.

Art activity
- Support rolling out brown coloured playdough and cutting it into squares. Use tools to make the surface look like toast.
- Add shaped playdough to look like a spread.
- Talk about how the children can create different textures.
- After baking, add more colour, using paints.

Extension/variation
- Arrange a still life of breakfast items using the playdough toast. Add a playdough knife and plate to the composition. Photograph it.

Links to home
- Ask parents to talk to their child about meal times and allow them to spread their own bread.

Related activities
- Teddy's birthday party (see page 75)
- Eat your greens (see page 88)
- A nice cup of tea (see page 101)
- Wedding project (see pages 117–120)

Fast food

Communication

(King's breakfast project)

• • • • • • • • • •

Learning objectives

Class

● To tap out simple repeated rhythms and make some up
● To explore how the sound of percussion instruments can be changed

What to do

Circle time

● Talk about favourite foods such as burgers and chips. Explain what is meant by 'fast food'.

Music activity

● Say the chant 'Yellow Butter' very slowly at first.
● Ask the children to clap with the beat, first one beat for 'Yellow Butter', etc.
● Speed up the rhyme but still with one beat.
● Support language development: *beat*, *pulse*, *tempo*.
● Ask which instrument sounds could accompany the four foods (butter, jelly, jam, bread). Ask for reasons.
● Hand out the instruments and let the children experiment. Let them practise making the sound to the beat.
● Divide the group into butter, jelly, jam, bread teams.
● When the practitioner reads the chant, the appropriate team shakes/hits their instrument.
● Play faster.

Extension/variation

● Make up a chant of different foods and play the instruments to the rhythms of the words.

Related activity

● Sing a song of soap (see page 52)

Resources

■ Chant: 'Yellow Butter' by Mary Ann Hoberman, from *This Little Puffin* compiled by Elizabeth Matterson (Puffin)
■ Percussion instruments

Not fussy

Communication

(King's breakfast project)

● ● ● ● ● ● ● ● ●

Resources

■ Poem: *The King's Breakfast* by A. A. Milne (Egmont Children's Books)

Learning objective

● To join in with imaginative role play during the narration of *The King's Breakfast*

What to do

Circle time

● Make sure there is room between the seated children for them to move their arms.
● Read *The King's Breakfast.*
● Ask how they would behave if they wanted something, like an ice cream, and they were told that they could not have it.
● Explain that you want the children to say the words from the poem – 'Fancy!' 'Oh!' 'Bother!' 'Oh, deary me!' 'Nobody' 'There, there!' 'Butter, eh?' as expressively as they can.
● Ask the children to use their arms, hands and facial expressions to add to their voices. Give them some examples.
● Practise the mimes with the words.
● Agree on a hand signal for the children to join in with the words.
● Read the poem and the children chorus the words.
● Divide the group into four: King, Queen, dairymaid, cow.
● Act out the story, each group taking it in turn.

Extension/variation

● Play 'Pass Me the Butter, Please'. Say 'Pass me the butter, please' in different voices, eg loud, soft, squeaky, etc, as a parcel is passed round the circle.

Class

Favourite meal

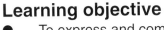

Learning objective
- To express and communicate their ideas, thoughts and feelings about their favourite meal

What to do

Circle time
- Read *The King's Breakfast*. Discuss that the King's favourite breakfast was bread and butter.
- Ask each child what is their favourite meal.
- Sing 'Bread and Jam', adding their favourite food to the song.
- Ask the children to mime eating their favourite meal.

Art activity
- Ask the children to produce a painting, sculpture, collage or still life installation to represent their favourite meal.
- As the children work, talk about the suitability of the materials they have chosen to represent the parts of the art work.
- Encourage the mixing of media, eg adding sand to paint to get a rough texture, using rubbings of string under the paper to represent spaghetti, etc.
- Talk about the shapes, texture, form and colours used.
- Talk about which media they prefer to work with, giving reasons.

Show and tell activity
- Encourage the group to talk about each other's work in positive terms.

Extensions/variations
- Encourage the children to identify where their ideas worked well.
- Ask the children to suggest where they can improve their work next time.

Links to home
- Ask parents to encourage their child to describe textures, shapes and colours of food.

Related activities
- Fruitful (see page 26) for papier-mâché
- Tooth fairy beads (see pages 28–29) for playdough
- Autumn leaves (see page 35) for printing

Resources
- Poem: *The King's Breakfast* by A. A. Milne (Egmont Children's Books)
- Song: 'Bread and Jam', from *This Little Puffin* compiled by Elizabeth Matterson (Puffin)
- Playfood (see EDUZONE, page 172)
- Plates, dishes, plastic knives, forks and spoons
- Resources as requested by children for art activity

Communication

(Creepy crawlies project)

• • • • • • • • •

Resources

- Rhymes: 'Little Miss Muffet', 'Incy Wincy Spider', from *This Little Puffin* compiled by Elizabeth Matterson (Puffin)
- Poem: 'The Spider and the Fly' by Mary Howitt, from *The Oxford Treasury of Children's Poems* (Oxford University Press)
- Card
- Scissors
- Pencils
- Crayons
- PVA glue and spreaders

• • • • • • • • • • •

Supervise the use of scissors.

Learning objectives

- To develop a repertoire of actions by putting a sequence of movements together
- To use lines to enclose a space, then begin to use these shapes to represent objects
- To use ideas involving fitting and overlapping

What to do

Music activity

- Sing the nursery rhymes and read the poem and do the actions.
- Talk about the children's experiences with spiders.

Craft activity

- Make pop-up spider cards. The children will need your support with folding and drawing on the correct edge of the paper.
- Fold a thin piece of card three times to get eight columns. Open the card out to a single fold.
- Draw half a spider, with four legs, with body and feet as shown. Cut out the spider.

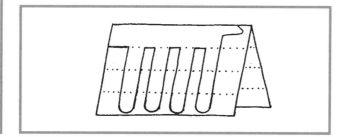

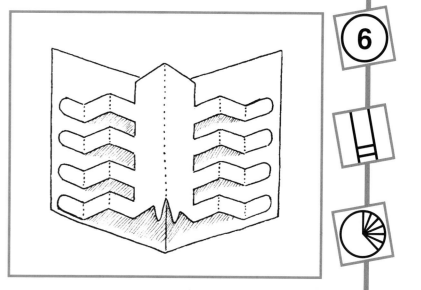

- Fold the card again so the legs are bent with the knees uppermost.
- Stick the feet down on to another piece of card so that when the card is opened the spider can pop up.
- Encourage the children to talk about their creations.

Extension/variation

- Decorate the cover of the card.

Links to home

- Ask parents to look for spiders' webs with their child.

Related activities

- What has eaten the lettuce? (see page 79)
- Homes for creepy crawlies (see page 85)

Slow as a snail

Communication

(Creepy crawlies project)

• • • • • • • • • •

Learning objective

- To explore an experience using a range of senses

Preparation

- Collect snails from the garden. Put them in a clear container. Feed the snails on lettuce before bringing into the setting. Return the snails to the garden after the session.

What to do

Collection table

- Let the children observe the snails.
- Support language development: *shell*, *slime*, *mollusc*, *slow*.

Dance activity

- Play the song and ask if the music is fast or slow (tempo), and why.
- Dance to the song 'The Snail'. Move each limb slowly.
- Contrast with a fast piece of music such as *Flight of the Bumble Bee*.

Extensions/variations

- Read the poem 'Animal Houses'.
- Make snails from coiled playdough.

Related activity

- What has eaten the lettuce? (see page 79)

Resources

- Song: 'The Snail' by Mary O'Hara (Levi-O'Hara) from *Music Speaks Louder than Words*
- Music: *Flight of the Bumble Bee* by Nikolai Rimsky-Korsakov (1844–1908)
- Poem: 'Animal Houses' by James Reeves, from *The Oxford Treasury of Children's Poems* (Oxford University Press)
- Live snails in clear box
- Magnifying glass
- Playdough (see page 29)
- CD player and tape recorder

• • • • • • • • • •

 Care with hygiene – do not handle snails. Wash hands before and after working outside. Check children have had a tetanus inoculation.

Monster insects

Communication
(Creepy crawlies project)

• • • • • • • • • •

Resources
- Poem: 'The Fly' by Walter de la Mare, from *The Oxford Treasury of Children's Poems* (Oxford University Press)
- Nonfiction books showing insects
- Junk materials
- Glue and spreaders
- Paints
- Paintbrushes
- Any other materials requested
- Scissors

• • • • • • • • • • • •

 Supervise the use of scissors.

Learning objective
- To express and communicate their ideas by using their imagination in art and design and stories

What to do
Circle time
- Read 'The Fly', which describes a fly's eye view of the world, ie everything looks very big. Suggest to the children that they imagine a very large insect. Ask them to describe their insect and what it would do.

Art activity
- Make or paint a monster insect.
- Remember it has to have six legs and three parts to its body. It can have two, four or no wings.
- Suggest the children look at books for some ideas.
- Encourage the children to talk about their creation.
- Encourage the children to make up a story about their monster insect.

Related activities
- What has eaten the lettuce? (see page 79)
- Homes for creepy crawlies (see page 85)

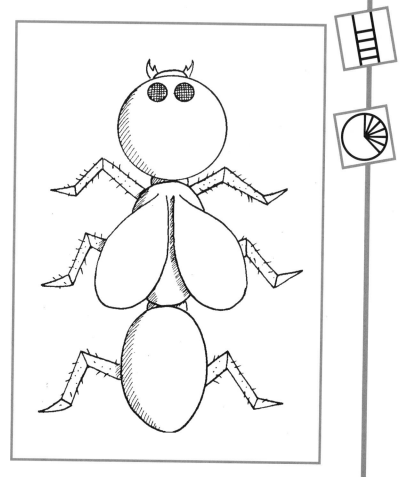

Wiggly worms

Learning objective
- To try to capture experiences using a variety of materials and ways

Preparation
- Dig up some earthworms as spares.

What to do

Outside activity
- Supervise collecting worms from the garden.
- Water ground with soapy water to encourage the worms to come to the surface. Rinse the worms in clean water.

Table activity
- Look at the bristles on a worm with the magnifying glass.
- Place worm on stiff paper and listen – you should hear the scraping of the bristles.
- Draw a worm.
- Make a wormery by putting layers of soil and sand into the jars. Put green leaves and some worms on top. Label with date and child's name. The worms will mix up the soil and sand.

Art activity
- Make worms from playdough, or thread pasta or cotton reels on to string.

Music activity
- Pretend to be wriggly worms.
- Make sounds representing the movement of a worm using scrapers or sandpaper blocks.
- Make up a worm dance using the instruments to set the rhythm and beat.

Extension/variation
- Learn the words of 'Nobody Loves Me'.

Related activities
- What has eaten the lettuce? (see page 79)
- Homes for creepy crawlies (see page 85)

Resources
- Trowels; spade or fork for adult; bucket of water; washing-up liquid; water; soil; sand; clear plastic jars; grass; other green leaves; apple core, etc; labels
- Earthworms
- Magnifying glass
- Song: ' Nobody Loves Me', from *This Little Puffin* compiled by Elizabeth Matterson (Puffin)
- Pencils and crayons
- White paper
- Playdough
- Pasta or cotton reels
- String
- Scrapers or sandpaper blocks

 Wash hands after working outside. Check children have had a tetanus inoculation.

Sick

Communication

(Teddy is ill project)

• • • • • • • • • •

Resources

- Story: 'Sick', from *Out and About Through the Year* by Shirley Hughes (Walker Books)
- Playdough or self-hardening clay
- Paints
- Paintbrushes
- Plastic knives
- Rolling pin
- Tools to make textures
- Varnish (for use by practitioner)

• • • • • • • • • •

 Use plastic knives for safety reasons.

Learning objective
- To capture an experience by making a model of a patient in bed

Preparation
- Make up playdough (see page 29)

What to do

Circle time
- Read 'Sick', and show the illustrations. How is the little girl feeling?
- Encourage the children to talk about when they were ill in bed.
- Ask how they felt. Suggest that the children make a person in bed from playdough or self hardening clay.

Craft activity
- Explain that they are going to use the 'slab technique'.
- Roll out the playdough to an even thickness. Cut out rectangles for the bed base, headboard and footboard (you might need to point out that these should be the same width). A small slab can be rolled up to make a pillow. Cut a wider piece to make a blanket.
- Make a person from rolls of dough. You could make the feet poke out of the bottom of the bed.
- Talk about how the children are making their sculpture.
- Paint in appropriate colours when hardened.
- Practitioner to varnish the sculptures.

Extension/variation
- Use tools to make the sculpture have a texture.

Links to home
- Ask parents to talk to their child about how they felt when they were ill.

Related activities
- Atishoo (see page 27)
- Tooth fairy beads (see pages 28–29)
- Losing a tooth (see page 87)
- I want to be . . . (see page 143)

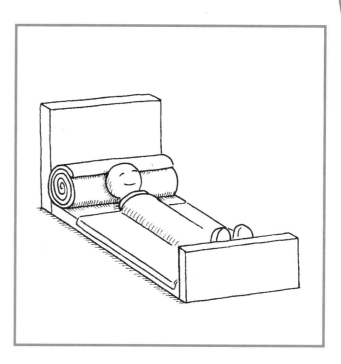

Gargle

Learning objectives
- To sing a few simple, familiar songs from memory
- To communicate their thoughts and feelings through songs

What to do
Circle time
- Who has been away from the setting because they were ill?
- Was it anything bad? How did they feel?
- Did anyone have a cold or flu?
- What should you do if you are going to sneeze? (Use a handkerchief.)
- Ask if anyone had a sore throat. Ask if they had to gargle with salt water or medicine.
- Let everyone try to make gargling noises (you don't need any water).
- Introduce the word *pitch* (high or low note) and gargle at a high note followed by a low note.

Music activity
- Sing the songs about being ill.
- Note which children are able to sing the songs from memory.
- Learn the actions for 'John Brown's Baby'.
- Which song was sad, which song was funny?
- Ask which song was their favourite. Ask for reasons for their choice.

Links to home
- Warn parents that children will be gargling!

Related activity
- Atishoo (see page 27)

Resources
- Tuned instrument, eg xylophone, glockenspiel or chime bars
- Songs: 'Miss Polly Had a Dolly', 'My Dolly Has to Stay in Bed', 'John Brown's Baby Has a Cold Upon its Chest', from *This Little Puffin* compiled by Elizabeth Matterson (Puffin)

© Mavis Brown
www.brilliantpublications.co.uk

Teddy is ill

Communication

(Teddy is ill project)

• • • • • • • • • •

Resources

- Book: *Teddybears and the Cold Cure* by Susanna Gretz and Alison Sage (A & C Black)
- For home corner: plates, cups, spoons; bed and bedding; box of handkerchiefs; plastic bottle of drink and plastic beaker
- Teddy or doll in pyjamas
- Tray, plastic beaker and jug
- Small cuddly toy
- Bowl of real fruit
- Poem: 'Schoolitis' by Brian Patten from *The Orchard Book of Funny Poems* (Orchard)

Learning objective

- To use their imagination to nurse an ill teddy or doll in the home corner, using available resources

What to do

Circle time

- Read *Teddybears and the Cold Cure*.
- What did the bear do when it got a cold?
- What do you do when you get a cold?
- What cheered up the teddy?
- What should you do so you do not catch a cold? Teach hygiene. Encourage children to use a handkerchief to wipe their noses, and to put their hand over their mouth when coughing and sneezing.
- Ask what they should have in the home corner if they made it like a bedroom for an ill teddy or doll.

Home corner

- With the children, set up the home corner like a bedroom for a doll or teddy that is ill.
- Set up a tray with beaker and jug for a drink. Does Teddy want his favourite toy to cuddle?
- Let the children play in groups of four in the home corner, looking after Teddy.
- Encourage the children to adapt materials to use, eg rolled paper as a thermometer (or strip of paper), tubing as stethoscope for doctor.
- Either act as doctor or ask who is playing the part.

Extensions/variations

- Have some fruit at snack time.
- Read 'Schoolitis', and ask if the little boy is really ill.

Links to home

- Ask parents to encourage hygiene when their child sneezes and coughs.

Related activities

- Atishoo (see page 27)
- I want to be . . . (see page 143)

I feel ill

Communication

(Teddy is ill project)
• • • • • • • • • •

Learning objective
- To express and communicate in a variety of ways how they felt when they were ill

What to do
Circle time
- Read *The Check Up* and ask if anyone has been to see the doctor.
- Ask the children to paint a picture or make up some music to illustrate how they felt about being ill.

Art activity
- As the children work, talk about what they are painting.
- Ask about the colours and shapes they are using and how they represent how they felt.

Music activity
- Ask whether the music should be slow or fast, high or low, loud or quiet to represent how they felt.
- Ask whether the tuned instruments or those with only one note give them their desired effect.
- Help the children to record their work.

Show and tell activity
- Encourage the group to talk about each other's work in positive terms.

Extensions/variations
- Encourage the children to identify where their ideas worked well.
- Ask the children to suggest where they can improve their work next time.

Links to home
- Check with parents whether their child has stayed in hospital.

Related activities
- Atishoo (see page 27)
- I want to be . . . (see page 143)

Resources
- Story: *The Check Up* by Helen Oxenbury (Walker Books)
- Paintbrushes
- Paints
- Junk material
- Sugar paper
- Variety of instruments including tuned instruments
- Tape recorder

Who's broken my chair?

Communication

(Goldilocks project)

● ● ● ● ● ● ● ● ● ●

Resources

- Story: *Goldilocks and the Three Bears* (Ladybird does a nice edition)
- Different chairs from the setting
- Catalogues with pictures of different designs and functions of chairs including throne, office chair, deck chair, garden chair
- Small-world figure with jointed legs
- Playdough
- Cardboard
- Balsa wood
- PVA glue and spreader
- Fabric
- Sponge squares
- Interlocking bricks
- Paper and crayons or pencils
- Papier-mâché
- Pipe cleaners
- Small cardboard boxes
- Scissors

● ● ● ● ● ● ● ● ● ●

 Supervise the use of scissors.

Learning objective

- To design and make a model chair for Goldilocks using different media

What to do

Circle time

- Read *Goldilocks and the Three Bears*.
- Ask children to sit in the different chairs and say if they are comfortable or not. Support language development: *hard*, *soft*, *bouncy*.
- Talk about the function of different chairs, eg adjustable office chair. Show catalogues with pictures of different types of chairs.
- Talk about different materials.
- Ask why Goldilocks broke Baby Bear's chair. (She was too heavy.)
- Suggest designing and making a chair for Goldilocks.

Craft activity

- Encourage the children to design and make a small chair for a small-world person, choosing the material and method themselves.
- Support language development for parts of a chair, eg *leg*, *seat*, *back*, *back rest*.
- Ask the children to think about how the chair is used, eg school chairs that children use every day need to be strong, portable and stackable.

- Talk about their intentions, discussing size and comfort. Ask how high it will be from the ground and why. How big will the seat be?

- After drawing their ideas on paper first, let the children construct a scale-model chair from suitable materials.
- Show the children techniques for:
  - ◆ making three-dimensional shapes
  - ◆ stiffening paper and card, eg rolling, folding and layering

  - ◆ joining, eg glue, tape, using paper clips, etc.

Extension/variation

- Make a bed for Teddy.

Links to home

- Ask parents to talk about different chairs and their qualities.

Related activities

- Porridge (see page 22)
- Sick (see page 129)

The three bears

Learning objective
- To make up a dance and musical accompaniment to mime the Goldilocks story

Preparation
- Find music on CD.

What to do
Circle time
- Read *Goldilocks and the Three Bears*.

Music activity
- Ask the children to select the sound of an instrument to represent the four characters, eg drum for Daddy Bear, bells for Goldilocks.
- Get the children to play the instrument when the character is mentioned.

Dance activity
- Play the music and ask the children to try to match the parts of the music to the story.
- There is a repeated 'Who's been sitting in my chair?' motif. Ask children to put up their hands when they hear this motif.
- Other parts of the music to listen for include:
  - knocking on the door (1.12 minutes)
  - the bears' arrival (2.42 minutes)
  - their anger (deep trombones and drums) (3.3 minutes)
  - the end of the piece, which sounds as though they try to make friends but ends with a chase.

- Ask the children to mime the story as Goldilocks, then as the bears, first without the music, then with the music.
- Support by giving instructions to the part of the story they are to mime.

Extensions/variations
- Divide the children into groups of four according to the children's abilities.
- A confident child can be Goldilocks to enact the story to the music.
- Learn the words to the song.
- Record the performance with camcorder and still camera.

Links to home
- Invite parents to watch the performance.

Related activities
- Porridge (see page 22)
- Peter and the Wolf (see page 44)
- Sick (see page 129)

Resources
- Story: *Goldilocks and the Three Bears* (Ladybird does a nice edition)
- Percussion instruments
- Music: *The Three Bears Phantasy* by Eric Coates (1886–1957)
- CD player or tape recorder
- Song: 'Goldilocks', from *High Low Dolly Pepper* by Veronica Clark (A & C Black)
- Camcorder
- Camera

Break in

Communication

(Goldilocks project)

● ● ● ● ● ● ● ● ●

Resources

■ Story: *Goldilocks and the Three Bears*
(Ladybird does a nice edition)

Learning objectives

● To play cooperatively as part of a group to act out the story of Goldilocks
● To use their imagination in stories

What to do

Circle time

● Read the story *Goldilocks and the Three Bears*.
● Stop the story just as the bears find Goldilocks in Baby Bear's bed.
● Ask the children whether the bears were angry. Would the children be angry to find someone had got into their room and broken their toys? Ask what they would say, and how they would look.
● Ask what the bears could have done to stop Goldilocks getting into their house. (They had not locked their door!)
● Ask them what might happen next. Encourage children to ask questions starting with *who*, *what*, *when*, *where*, *why* and *how*.
● Ask what excuse Goldilocks could give for her actions.

Extension/variation

● Pretend they are newspaper reporters and visit the three bears to get the story.

Related activities

● Porridge (see page 22)
● Sick (see page 129)

Class

Goldilocks and the three bears

Learning objectives

Class
- To respond to comments and questions, entering into dialogue about what they did in the Goldilocks project and voicing preferences
- To show evidence that they have responded in a variety of creative ways to the topic

Preparation

- This activity should be done at the end of the Goldilocks project. Make a display of the children's work from the other activities. Include photographs.

What to do

Show and tell

- Show the video of the children's performance to remind them of what they did.
- Go round the circle and ask each child to show and tell about what they have created for the Goldilocks project.
- Ask which activity they liked best.

Extension/variation

- If appropriate ask how they could have improved what they had created.

Links to home

- Invite parents to see the group's work.

Related activities

- Porridge (see page 22)
- Sick (see page 129)

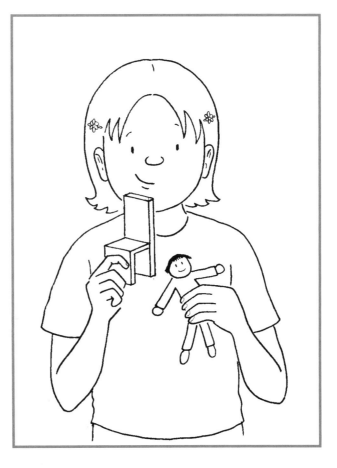

Resources

- Children's work
- Video of performance
- Television and video player
- Photograph display of work
- Book: *Goldilocks and the Three Bears* (Ladybird does a nice edition)

I don't use these now

Communication

(Growing up project)

• • • • • • • • • •

Resources

- Book: *The Last Noo-Noo* by Jill Murphy (Walker Books)
- Toys and items used by babies for collection table
- Small table with plain table cloth (not white)
- Digital or polaroid camera
- Paper
- Paints
- Paintbrushes

Learning objectives

- To make a still life arrangement of items used by a baby
- To explore the colour, texture, shape, form and space of the arrangement

Preparation

- The children should have had experience in arranging items (still life or installations).

What to do

Circle time

- Read *The Last Noo-Noo* and talk about the things that the children do not use any more. Ask the children for examples.
- Show the children items from the collection table. Let them examine the items and talk about them, eg *dummy*, *rattles*, *potty*, *feeding bottle*.
- What is the shape and texture of each item? Does it make a noise? Could a baby chew it?
- Support language development: *smooth*, *soft*, *hard*, *jingle*.

Art activity

- Suggest that the children select three to five items that they no longer use, and to place them into a still life arrangement on the small table.
- Let them photograph the arrangement from all four sides.

- Discuss whether all the items can be seen from each angle.
- Point out the shapes the items make with each other and the shapes made by the spaces between the items.

Extension/variation

- Let the children paint pictures of their still life arrangement.

Links to home

- Ask parents for items to donate or borrow. (Remind them to put name labels on.)

Baby games

● ● ● ● ● ● ● ● ● ●

Class

Learning objective
● To join in with simple songs

What to do
Circle time
● Read one of the stories.
● Ask if anyone has a younger brother or sister. Ask how they felt when they first saw their new brother/sister.

Music activity
● Ask the children if they sing songs to their younger brother or sister.
● Can they remember the songs that they learned when they were babies?
● Ask children to volunteer to sing a song for a baby and describe the actions.
● Learn some baby game songs, with the children doing the actions with their toy.
● Suggest they can now sing songs to their younger siblings.

Extensions/variations
● Invite a parent who has a new baby to stay for a while in the setting and to talk to the children about the baby.
● Suggest that the children sing to the baby. Sing a lullaby such as 'Rock a Bye Baby'.

Related activities
● Family fingers (see page 50)
● Ring around (see page 64)
● Tra-la (see page 65)

Resources
■ Book: *New Born* by Kathy Henderson (Frances Lincoln)
■ Book: *Little Brother and the Cough* by Hiawyn Oram (Frances Lincoln) – alternative title
■ Rhyme: 'Baby Games', from *This Little Puffin* compiled by Elizabeth Matterson (Puffin)
■ Song: 'Rock a Bye Baby', from *The I Can't Sing Book* by Jackie Silberg (Brilliant Publications)
■ Teddies and dolls

© Mavis Brown
www.brilliantpublications.co.uk

Communication

(Growing up project)

• • • • • • • • • •

Resources

- Book: *When I Was a Baby* by Catherine Anholt (Picture Mammoth)
- For home corner, set up as a nursery: baby dolls, larger dolls
- For water play: plastic dolls, towels, flannels and soap
- Action song: 'We've Grown So Tall', from *Start with a Song* by Mavis de Mierre (Brilliant Publications)

• • • • • • • • • •

Supervise the water tray activity.

Learning objectives

- To enjoy stories based on themselves
- To use representation as a means of communication

What to do

Circle time

- Read *When I Was a Baby* and discuss each picture. Compare what the children can do now, with what they could not do as a baby.
- Support language development: *how old?* *baby*, *toddler*, *child*.
- Ask the children if they could describe their earliest memory. Begin, 'I can remember when . . .'
- End the session with the song 'We've Grown So Tall'.
- Ask what the children think they will be able to do next year.

Home corner

- As the children play with the dolls, ask them how old the baby is, and what it can do. Relate the questions to the story.
- Supervise imaginative play and support language development.

Water tray

- Supervise imaginative play and support language development at the water tray as the children play at bathing the dolls.

Extensions/variations

- Invite a parent with a young baby to visit the setting. Talk about what the baby can do, and what it cannot do. The parent could show the children how to feed and bath the baby.
- Talk about how to be safe when a baby is around, eg keep small toys away from the baby as babies often put everything into their mouths.

My favourite things

• • • • • • • • • •

Learning objectives
• To respond in a variety of ways to what they see, hear, smell, touch and feel
• To make a mobile displaying representations of their favourite things

Preparation
• The children need to understand that they can make a model of an item rather than use the actual item in their art work.

What to do
Circle time
• Read *Almost Famous Daisy,* who travels the world to find out what her favourite things are, so she can enter a painting competition.

Show and tell activity
• Ask each child to show their favourite thing, eg food/colour/T-shirt, and explain why they like it so much.
• Ask the other children to comment on each other's choices.
• Support language development: *like, enjoy, favourite, best.*

Home corner
• Let the children play with their favourite toy.

Wet playtime
• Watch a favourite video.
• Ask why the children enjoyed the video.

Art activity
• Make a mobile of five items (can be all the same) hanging from a clothes hanger.
• Ask what media they are going to use.
• First make models of items using a chosen medium, eg playdough, papier-mâché or photographs covered with plastic. Do not mix media as the mobile will not balance.
• Support and encourage problem-solving.
• Photograph the finished mobile.

Extension/variation
• Children can use actual items to make a mobile if they have chosen small disposable items, eg tubes of sweets.

Links to home
• Ask parents to allow their child to bring a favourite item. Advise them to label it to indicate its owner.
• Ask parents to let child have photographs (non-returnable) of people/pets/items/places their child likes.

Related activities
• Fruitful (see page 26) for papier-mâché
• Tooth fairy beads (see pages 28–29) for playdough

Resources
■ Book: *Almost Famous Daisy* by Richard Kidd (Frances Lincoln)
■ Video player and television
■ Wire clothes hangers
■ Thin string or thread
■ Photographs (non-returnable) of things they like (for mobile)
■ Sticky-back plastic or laminator
■ Playdough
■ Papier-mâché
■ Paper, paints and paintbrushes
■ Camera
■ Scissors

• • • • • • • • • •

 Supervise the use of scissors.

Badges

Communication

(Who is knocking? project)

• • • • • • • • •

Resources

■ Book: *ABC I Can Be* by Verna Allette Wilkins (Tamarind Books)
■ Pictures of people wearing clothes that identify their job, eg police, firefighter, postal delivery person, etc
■ Playdough or self-hardening clay (see page 29)
■ Tool for cutting, eg a blunt bodkin in a cork
■ Safety pins or brooch backs
■ Tape
■ Strong glue (for practitioner)
■ Rolling pin
■ Paints and paintbrushes
■ Diluted PVA glue for glazing

• • • • • • • • • •

 Supervise use of cutting tool and safety pins and/or brooch backs.

Learning objective
● To show an interest in making a badge of initial letters

What to do
Circle time
● Show picture book *ABC I Can Be* and show the pictures and photographs.
● Ask how they would know if a policeman/electricity meter reader/postal delivery person had come to their door (uniform and badge).

Craft activity
● Help the children to make identity badges of their initials from playdough or self-hardening clay.
● Roll out a thin sausage of material. Shape into letters.
● Roll out a slab of material and wet it. Place the letters on top and press down gently to keep the letters in relief.
● Alternatively, inscribe the letters into the slab.
● Cut round the letters to make a badge.
● After baking, paint the base and the separate letters with no more than three colours.
● When dry, glaze with dilute PVA glue.
● When the glaze is dry, support sticking the pin on the back of the badge.

Extension/variation
● Make a badge with a word such as 'Gas'.

Links to home
● Ask parents if they could talk to their child about the job they do, and if they have to wear a uniform, special clothes or identity badge.

Related activity
● Tiles (see page 36)

Knock, knock

Communication

(Who is knocking? project)

● ● ● ● ● ● ● ● ●

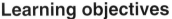

Class

Learning objectives
● To build a repertoire of songs
● To capture experiences by making up simple songs

What to do
Circle time
● Read *Alfie Gets in First*. Ask who came to help Alfie's mum to get back into their house.
● Ask who else might call at their home.
● Talk about safety, and that they should not answer the door without their parents' permission.

Music activity
● Use finger puppets of different people who help us.
● Sing '(Patrick) Was a Postman', substituting the name of a child in the group, preferably one whose name starts with 'P'. Give the child the puppet. Ask what the postman is wearing.
● Sing the song with the children, using the instruments to keep the beat.
● Choose another puppet and ask what it is wearing. Ask if that person would knock on the child's door at home and what he/she does.

● With the children make up a suitable line with the same beat, eg 'Martin was a milkman . . . He delivered all the milk . . .'

Extensions/variations
● Ask the children who else helps them, eg to cross the road. Give the child the puppet and encourage the child to sing the first verse as 'I am a lollipop man/lady . . .'
● Sing 'I Went to School One Morning' and make up additions 'I saw a . . . (big strong dustman and he went like this, and do the actions).

Links to home
● Ask parents to talk about officials who come to their home.

Extensions/variations
● Hats (see page 32)
● Homes topic

Resources
■ Book: *Alfie Gets in First* by Shirley Hughes (Walker Books)
■ Nonfiction books showing different careers
■ Finger puppets of different people who help us (NES, see page 172)
■ Songs: 'Patrick Was a Postman', 'I Went to School One Morning', from *This Little Puffin* compiled by Elizabeth Matterson (Puffin)
■ Percussion instruments

Communication

(Who is knocking? project)

• • • • • • • • • •

Resources

■ Items that can be associated with a person's job, eg milk bottle = person who delivers milk, letter and parcel = post person, bucket and chamois leather or wiper = window cleaner, newspaper = person who delivers the newspaper and magazines, stethoscope = doctor, etc

■ Book: *What Am I?* by Debbie MacKinnon and Anthea Sieveking (Frances Lincoln)

■ Nonfiction books showing different careers

■ Clothes and items suitable to represent people who help us

• • • • • • • • • •

⚠ Ensure correct child:adult ratio for visit.

Learning objectives

● To make comparisons between different jobs
● To play cooperatively as part of a small group to act out a narrative

What to do

Circle time

● Show the items and ask the children who would use them. Ask what the person would do. Support language development, eg doctors make people better when they are ill.
● Read and show *What Am I?* and talk about the jobs illustrated.
● Ask what job the children would like to do when they grow up. Ask for reasons.
● Ask the children what job they would not like to do. Ask them for reasons. Challenge racist or sexist remarks.
● Ask them to mime what the person would do.

Role playing

● Encourage the children to dress up and say which job they are representing.
● Encourage the children to make up a role play activity involving them as the person helping another. Support language development.

Extensions/variations

● Organize a visitor, eg a police officer, to talk about how they can help children.
● Organize a visit, eg to the fire station.

Links to home

● Ask parents if they can support a visit.
● Ask parents to come and talk about their job. Ask them to bring things to show the children.

Related activities

● Hats (see page 32)
● Losing a tooth (see page 87)
● Teddy is ill project (see pages 129–132)

④

A load of rubbish

Learning objectives
- To explore the texture of materials
- To express and communicate their ideas, thoughts and feelings about litter

Preparation
- Access the word processing program in the computer.

What to do

Circle time
- Read *Tidy up Titch*. Ask where Titch should put stuff he did not want any more.
- Talk about getting rid of rubbish.
- Ask what should happen to it. (They might suggest: cleaner pick it up/person should not have dropped it/should have put it in the bin.)

Table activity
- Support sorting different materials into types and discuss the different textures.
- Support language development: *smooth, rough, shiny, transparent, plastic, metal, paper, fabric, wood, stone, natural* and *man-made*.

Art activity
- Encourage the children to make a collage from the litter material as part of a 'Don't drop litter' poster.

Computer activity
- Support printing the text for the poster using a word processing package on a computer. Let the children choose the font.

Extension/variation
- Take the children on a walk to see the dustcart collecting rubbish.

Links to home
- Get permission for taking the children out of the setting. Ask for parents to help in the walk.
- If any households recycle their rubbish, ask that they take their child to the recycling bins.

Related activity
- Paper-making (see pages 24–25)

Resources
- Book: *Tidy up Titch* by Pat Hutchins (Red Fox)
- Clean discarded objects from the groups of materials – paper, plastic, metal, wood, natural, man-made, recyclable
- Sugar paper
- PVA glue and spreaders
- Paints
- Paintbrushes
- Computer with word processing program
- Printer
- Paper for printing text

 Ensure there are no sharp edges on any of the objects. Wash hands after the activity. Check LEA regulations for taking children out of the setting.

© Mavis Brown
www.brilliantpublications.co.uk

Blossom

Communication
(The Selfish Giant project)

• • • • • • • • • •

Resources
- Book: *The Selfish Giant* by Oscar Wilde (Puffin)
- White and pink toilet tissue
- Liquid paper glue or PVA glue
- Scissors

• • • • • • • • • • •

 Supervise the use of scissors.

Learning objectives
- To explore texture and space when making paper blossoms
- To talk about the difficulty of the task

What to do
Circle time
- Read the part of the story when the trees blossom. Suggest that the children make flowers.

Craft activity
- To make blossoms, take one sheet of white or pink toilet tissue and fold it in half.
- Roll up loosely round the tip of the finger, and remove.

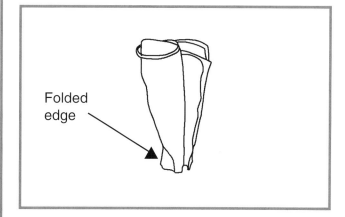

Folded edge

- Put two small spots of liquid paper glue (solid glue will tear) on the folded edge inside, and pinch this end together.

- While holding the edge, carefully cut down the length of the cylinder to make strips, starting at the outer edge of the coil, folding the petals back as you cut.
- Give support and encourage persistence.

④

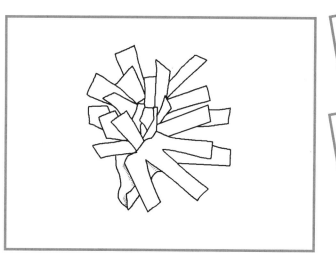

Extension/variation
- Use different coloured tissue and use the blossoms on a collage, wall display or part of the tree costumes (see page 93).

Links to home
- Ask parents to help their children make blossoms at home for the play.

Related activities
- Spring flowers (see page 34)
- Autumn leaves (see page 35)
- Trees (see page 93)

Peaches

Communication

(The Selfish Giant project)

● ● ● ● ● ● ● ● ●

Resources
- Book: *The Selfish Giant* by Oscar Wilde (Puffin)
- Chopping board
- Knife for practitioner
- Fresh peaches
- 150g yoghurt pots with hole in base
- Old saucers
- Compost
- Song: 'Here is My Head', from *Start with a Song* by Mavis de Mierre (Brilliant Publications)

Class

Learning objective
● To show an interest in the peach fruit, using a range of senses

What to do

Snack time
● Read *The Selfish Giant* up to the part that describes the peach trees in the garden.
● Pass round the peaches and let the children examine them.
● Ask them to describe them, how they feel, smell and their colour and texture.
● Ask what they think is inside the peach.
● Cut the peach in half. Keep the stones (the seeds) to plant.
● Let each child taste a piece. Ask them what it tastes like.

Cooking activity
● Bake a peachy tart (see page 147).

Extensions/variations
● Plant the peach seeds into compost.
● Let the children take turns in looking after the seeds/plants.
● Sing 'Here is My Head' but change 'apple' to 'peach'.

Links to home
● Encourage parents to discuss the appearance and texture of fruit.

Peachy tart

Seasons

Communication

(The Selfish Giant project)

• • • • • • • • • • •

Resources

- 4 yoghurt pots plain flour (= 125g)
- 1 yoghurt pot sunflower margarine (= 60g)
- 1/4 teaspoon salt
- 3/4 full pot of cold water (= 50ml)
- 1 ripe but firm peach (about 50g)
- 1 heaped teaspoonful sugar to sweeten
- Chopping board
- Knife
- Cooking tray
- Medium sized plate to cut round
- Fork
- Tablespoon/teaspoon
- Rolling pin
- Mixing bowl
- 50g yoghurt pot for measuring
- For meringue: 1 egg white, 1 yoghurt pot caster sugar (= 60g)

• • • • • • • • • • •

 An adult should put food in and out of the oven. Check for wheat allergy.

Learning objectives
- To explore the properties of pastry
- To explore the properties of meringue

What to do

How to make the pastry
- Using a 50g yoghurt pot allows the children to measure out the ingredients themselves.

Method
- Practitioner removes skin by pouring boiling water over peach. Let it stand for a few minutes until the skin comes away from the flesh. Remove the stone to examine and plant later. Chop up the peach.
- Mix the salt into the flour.
- Rub the fat into the flour until it looks like breadcrumbs. Ask the children how the flour and fat feel.
- Stir in the water, and knead until smooth. Add more flour if the mixture is sticky. Ask how different the breadcrumb mixture feels from the wet pastry.
- Roll out the pastry. Cut round the medium sized plate to make a circular base.
- Put the chopped up peach and some sugar on the pastry.
- Discuss how to complete the pastry, eg fold the pastry over the peaches, or cut strips of pastry and lay a lattice over, or cut another circle and lay on top, etc.

- Place on a well-greased baking tray.
- Cook in moderate oven 175°C/375°F/Gas Mark 5 for 10 to 15 minutes until golden brown.

Extensions/variations
- The pastry tart could be baked blind (without filling) as above and kept to the next day. Stew the peach for a short time with sugar until just soft, cool then arrange on top of pastry.

- Make a meringue to go on top. Let the children whisk the egg white (practitioner separates the yolk from the white) until stiff, then again while slowly adding 1 yoghurt pot of caster sugar. Ask the children to describe the texture of the meringue. Top the tart with meringue and place in slow oven 150°C/300°F/Gas Mark 2 for about 15 minutes until crisp on the top.

Links to home
- Ask for help with cooking.

© Mavis Brown
www.brilliantpublications.co.uk

Creative Development

The giant's garden

Communication
(The Selfish Giant project)
••••••••••

Learning objective
- To imitate and create movement in response to the music and story of *The Selfish Giant*

Preparation
- To help organize the music for this project, the recommended CD has all the tracks required.
- Each scene with the music should be practised on separate occasions. Speak the lines as the music is played to acquaint yourself with the rhythms and tempo of the music. Shorten the pieces if needed.

- **Scene 1**: Children in garden – 'Passepied' from *Suite Bergamasque*
- **Scene 2**: Giant returns – 'Danse Bohemienne' played loudly with bass turned up, then turn down for children playing in the road
- **Scene 3**: Winter in the giant's garden – 'Danse'
- **Scene 4**: Spring has come and giant gets out of bed – 'Arabesque 2'
- **Scene 5**: Giant knocks down the wall – children's percussion
- **Scene 6**: Children come to play – 'Passepied'
- **Scene 7**: The giant is old, and sees the Christ child for the last time – 'Nocturne'.

Resources
- Book: *The Selfish Giant* by Oscar Wilde (Puffin)
- Internet: search Selfish Giant Oscar Wilde
- CD: Debussy Piano Works Volume 1, pianist François-Joël Thiollier (Naxos 8.553290)
- CD player

The giant's garden (continued)

Communication

(The Selfish Giant project)

• • • • • • • • • •

What to do

Circle time

● Read *The Selfish Giant* and tell the children that they are going to act out the story to music.

● Play the music and talk about how it can fit into the story. Then play the music and read the story at the same time.

Dance activity

● As the music is played, ask the children to close their eyes as you read, and imagine that they are the children in the story.

● Ask the children to dance to the music, fitting their movements to the story line as you read.

● Repeat the process for each scene.

● Which piece of music is fast and which is slow?

● Which piece of music sounds happy, and which sounds sad?

● Ask for reasons for their choice.

Links to home

● Invite parents to watch the performance.

Related activities

● Bricks (see page 30)
● Freezing cold project (see pages 168–171)
● Seasons topic
● Gardening topic

Class

The Selfish Giant

Learning objective
- To use their imagination in art and design and music for the performance of *The Selfish Giant*

What to do

Circle time
- Read *The Selfish Giant.*

Art activity
- What could the giant look like? What should he wear? Make a large papier-mâché head for the giant (see Myself, page 31).
- What would the wall look like? What material would the giant use to build the wall? Decorate boxes.
- How should we dress the seasons? Draw designs of the costumes. Decorate dressing-up clothes.
- How could we show the trees bare, then growing blossom in the play? Make blossoms (see page 145).

Music activity
- What kind of sound could we make for the knocking down of the wall?
- What did the giant use? (An axe.)
- Explore the instruments or make one to create the sound.

Extensions/variations
- Encourage the children to choose their activity to contribute to the play.
- Put the scenes together with the scenery, props and giant costume, add the dialogue and put on a performance.

Links to home
- Ask parents to help their child to make a costume.
- Invite parents to watch the performance.

Related activities
- Bird masks (see page 16)
- Bricks (see page 30)
- Myself (see page 31)
- Spring flowers (see page 34)
- Autumn leaves (see page 35)
- Rattle those pans (see page 51)
- Trees (see page 93)
- Freezing cold project (see pages 168–171)

Communication
(The Selfish Giant project)

• • • • • • • • • •

Resources
- Book: *The Selfish Giant* by Oscar Wilde (Puffin)
- Internet: search Selfish Giant Oscar Wilde
- Newspaper
- Wallpaper paste (without fungicide)
- Chicken wire
- Cardboard boxes
- Lining paper
- Paints and brushes
- Crayons
- Percussion instruments
- Home-made instruments
- Junk material
- Colourful fabrics, Christmas decorations artificial flowers
- White and pink toilet paper
- Bodkins and thread
- Scissors
- PVA glue and spreaders

• • • • • • • • • •

 Supervise the use of sharp implements.

Coloured balloons

Communication

(Balloons project)

• • • • • • • • • •

Resources
- Paper
- Thick paints
- Sponges, brushes
- Coloured balloons of different shapes
- Scissors

• • • • • • • • • •

 Supervise the use of scissors.

Learning objectives
- To use their bodies to explore texture and space and differentiate marks and movements on paper
- To begin to differentiate colours
- To explore what happens when they mix colours

What to do

Circle time
- Talk about the colours and shapes of the balloons. Support language development: *round*, *circle*, *sphere*, *cylindrical*, *tube*.

Art activity
- Allow the children to paint with one colour using a variety of methods, eg finger paint, sponges, brushes of different sizes.
- Talk about the shapes they are making with their finger painting.
- Support language development: names of colours and equipment.
- The practitioner can either cut out balloon shapes or draw a balloon shape over the painting for the child to cut out.
- Add string and display on the wall.

Extension/variation
- Give the children two colours with which to experiment.

Links to home
- Ask parents to point out and name two-dimensional shapes.

Related activities
- Over the rainbow project (see pages 113–116)

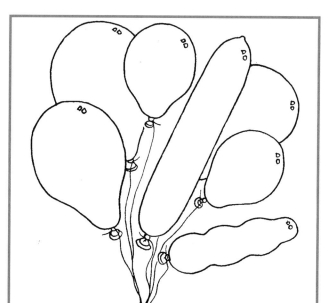

Pop

Communication
(Balloons project)
• • • • • • • • • •

Learning objective
- To explore and learn how sounds can be changed, using a balloon as the instrument

What to do
Circle time
- Read the story *Oriki and the Monster Who Hated Balloons.*
- Ask why the monster did not like balloons. Ask the children if they like balloons.
- Ask what kind of sound a balloon makes when it is burst. Is the sound loud or quiet?
- Ask them what is inside the balloon. What is the sound when the air comes out?

Music activity
- Ask the children to make the balloon make different sounds. Tell them to experiment on their own and not to disturb other children working on their ideas.
- Give out deflated balloons.
- Suggest putting dried peas inside.

Show and tell
- After experimentation, let each child show what sounds they can make with a balloon.
- Talk about the shapes they had to pull the balloon into to make the sounds.

Extensions/variations
- Make a shaker by using the balloon as the base. Cover with papier-mâché.
- When dry, split in half. Put in peas and reseal with more papier-mâché.
- Paint the outside.

Links to home
- Ask parents if their child is nervous of balloons.

Related activities
- Myself (see page 31) for shaker
- Running water (see page 71) for sound effects

Resources
- Book: *Oriki and the Monster Who Hated Balloons* by John Agard (Longman Book Project)
- Balloons
- Balloon pumps
- Dried peas (to put in balloons)
- Papier-mâché (no fungicide in the paste)
- Paints and paintbrushes

• • • • • • • • • •

⚠ A child could choke on a burst balloon. Use a pump to blow up balloons. Warn the children that the balloons will make a loud noise when they burst.

Silly balloons

Communication

(Balloons project)

● ● ● ● ● ● ● ● ● ●

Resources

■ Book: *The Blue Balloon* by Mick Inkpen (Hodder)
■ Sculpture balloons
■ Balloon pump

● ● ● ● ● ● ● ● ● ●

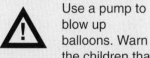 Use a pump to blow up balloons. Warn the children that the balloons will make a loud noise when they burst.

Learning objective

● To use one object to represent another, even when the objects have few characteristics in common

Preparation

● If possible, invite a performer who specializes in balloon sculpture.

What to do

Circle time

● Read *The Blue Balloon.*
● If you have a visitor, let them make different shapes with the balloons. If not, do it yourself.
● Ask, 'What shape is this balloon?'
● What could this balloon be? What could you do with it? For example, it could be a back scratcher, a hat, an animal.

Extensions/variations

Outside activity

● Let them play with the balloons outside.
● Supervise playground and balloons.

Links to home

● Ask parents if their child is nervous of balloons.
● Tell parents about the visitor, and ask for donations if appropriate.

Related activities

● Seaside project (see pages 160–163)

The red balloon

Communication

(Balloons project)

• • • • • • • • • •

Learning objectives
● To show an interest in what they see and hear
● To respond to music with body movement

What to do

Circle time
● Show the video *The Red Balloon*.
● Discuss the feelings of the little boy and ask the children to suggest what the 'feelings' of the balloon were. Talk to the red balloon.

Dance activity
● Play 'Arabesque 1' and encourage the children to pretend to chase a balloon floating away from them.

Extension/variation
● Let the children choose between some of the other activities in the Balloons project (see pages 151–153).

Links to home
● Have a balloon race during the annual fête, summer fair or sports day.

Related activity
● Musical colours (see page 115)

Resources
■ Video: *The Red Balloon* by Albert Lamorisse (1956) (Beaveworld 1992)
■ Video player and television
■ Music: 'Arabesque 1' by Claude Debussy (1862–1918) from *Debussy Piano Works Volume* 1 (Naxos 8.553290)
■ CD player
■ Large red balloon

• • • • • • • • • •

 A child could choke on a burst balloon.

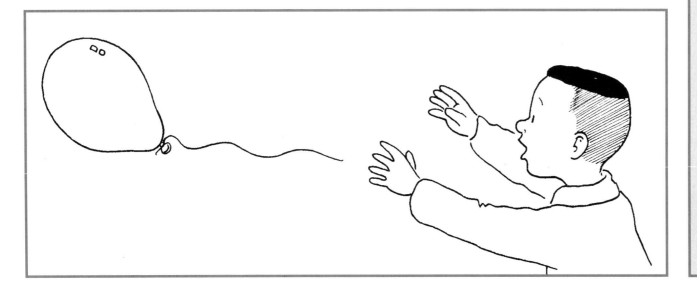

Dancing clown

Communication

(Nutcracker project)

• • • • • • • • •

Resources

- Book: *The Nutcracker* by Alexander Dumas translated by Douglas Munro (Oxford University Press)
- Photocopier
- Split pins
- Scissors
- Small hole punch
- Materials to decorate, eg sequins, tissue paper
- Wool
- Glue and spreaders
- Pencils
- Action song: 'I'm a Clown', from *Start with a Song* by Mavis de Mierre (Brilliant Publications)

• • • • • • • • •

 Supervise the use of scissors.

Learning objectives
- To make and decorate a moving toy
- To make comparisons

Preparation
- Read story of *The Nutcracker* to simplify it before telling it to the children.
- Photocopy this page on to card, one for each child.
- Make up one toy to show the lever movement.

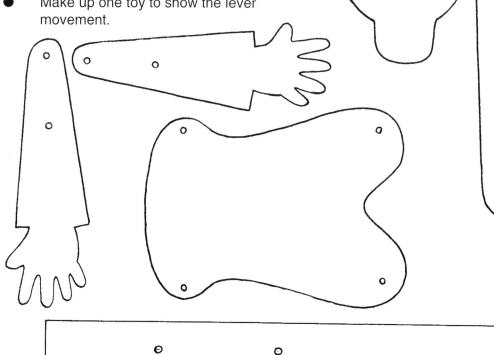

This page may be photocopied by the purchasing institution.

Dancing clown (continued)

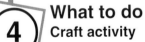

What to do
Craft activity
● Support cutting out of the shapes. Punch holes in the shapes for the split pins.
● Overlap the tops of the arms and tops of the legs and join to strip with split pin.
● Connect second set of holes to the body.
● Fit together so the strip can move freely up and down.
● Stick the head on to the top of the strip.
● Decorate the front. Add hair or a hat.
● Encourage the children to discuss how each clown looks different because of the decoration.

Music activity
● Sing the song 'I'm a Clown' while pushing the stick up and down.

Extension/variation
● Make a teddy bear or doll in the same way.

Related activities
● Toy soldiers (see page 37)
● Clowns (see page 97)

Communication

(Nutcracker project)

• • • • • • • • • •

Resources

- Book: *The Nutcracker* by Alexander Dumas, translated by Douglas Munro (Oxford University Press)
- Teddy bears with jointed limbs
- Music: *The Parade of the Wooden Soldiers* by Léon Jessel (1871–1942)
- Drum with stick for practitioner
- Percussion instruments
- Kazoo made from comb and paper
- Book for instruments to make: *The I Can't Sing Book* by Jackie Silberg (Brilliant Publications)
- Action song: 'Tarara Boomdeay', from *Start with a Song* by Mavis de Mierre (Brilliant Publications)
- CD player

Learning objective

- To learn to march to a beat like soldiers

What to do

Circle time

- Remind the children that Fritz in *The Nutcracker* liked playing with toy soldiers.
- Teach left and right. (Remember you are facing the children.)
- Let the children march the teddies on their knees to *The Parade of the Wooden Soldiers*.

Outside activity

- Use a drum to establish a beat, then vary the tempo.
- Encourage the children to march around in line, banging percussion instruments and playing kazoos, or combs with paper (see *The I Can't Sing Book*).

Extensions/variations

- Let the children make their own toy soldier.
- Learn the song 'Tarara Boomdeay' and sing and march to the tune.

Links to home

- Ask parents to bring in their child's teddy bear (with name label).
- Ask for spare combs (without tails).

Related activities

- Toy soldiers (see page 37)
- Musical toys (see page 67)
- Clowns (see page 97)

Class

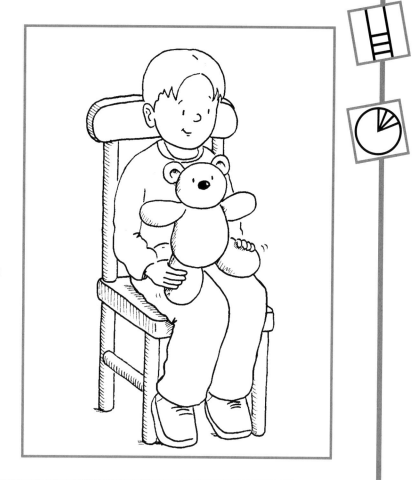

Only a dream

Learning objectives
- To imagine that toys can come alive
- To tap out some simple repeated rhythms

What to do

Circle time
- Read from Chapter 3 of *The Nutcracker*, when the toys come alive to fight the mice.
- Imagine their toy had come alive. What would the toy say? What would they do?
- Write down their ideas on the flip chart.

Music activity
- Let each child examine and play with a mechanical toy.
- Hand out the percussion instruments.
- Ask the children to make up a rhythm to copy the movement of the toy.

Extension/variation

Dance activity
- Let half the group play percussion rhythms while the other half move to the sounds and pretend to be toys. Swap places and repeat.

Related activities
- Toy soldiers (see page 37)
- Musical toys (see page 67)
- Clowns (see page 97)
- Rats (see page 105)

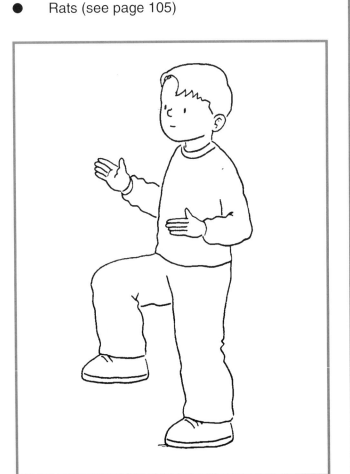

Resources
- Book: *The Nutcracker* by Alexander Dumas, translated by Douglas Munro (Oxford University Press)
- Flip chart
- Felt-tip pen
- Mechanical toys
- Percussion instruments

The Nutcracker Ballet

Communication

(Nutcracker project)

• • • • • • • • • •

Resources

- Video: *The Nutcracker* performed by the Kirov Ballet (Philips Video Classics)
- Book: *The Nutcracker* by Alexander Dumas, translated by Douglas Munro (Oxford University Press)
- Video: 'The Nutcracker Suite' in *Fantasia* (Walt Disney)
- Music: *The Nutcracker Suite* by Peter Tchaikovsky (1840–1893)
- Video player and television
- Ballet shoes
- Ballerina's tutu
- CD player

Learning objectives

- To show an interest in what they see, hear, touch and feel
- To try to capture experiences and responses with dance and make comparisons

Preparation

- Read the story and simplify it to retell the children. (The original story was by E. T. A. Hoffmann.)
- Check the story line of the ballet. (The familiar tunes are in Act 2.)

What to do

Circle time

- Watch the video *The Nutcracker* (performed by the Kirov Ballet). Explain the story as it is shown.
- When does the story take place? (Christmas Eve.)
- What kind of children are Marie and Fritz? What do they do to show their character? (Fritz breaks the Nutcracker and although he is an ugly toy Marie loves him and nurses him.)
- How does Marie help the Nutcracker to kill the Mouse King? (Throws her shoe at the Mouse King.)

- Explain that the Nutcracker is really a prince and Marie becomes his princess. They go to the prince's Kingdom of Sweets.
- At the end, was it a dream?

Collection table

- Let the children examine the short frilly skirt (tutu) and ballet shoes which help the ballerina to dance on the points of their toes.
- How are the ballerina's skirt and shoes different from their own clothes and shoes?

Dance activity

- Play the 'Dance of the Flowers', from *The Nutcracker Suite*. Ask the children to walk then run round the room to the music like the ballerinas.

Extension/variation

- Watch 'The Nutcracker Suite' section in the video *Fantasia* (14 minutes). Ask which video the children liked best, giving reasons.

Links to home

- Ask if any parents have ballet shoes and a tutu. Do any of the children go to ballet or dance classes?
- Ask if any parents have had ballet training and can give a demonstration.

Class

Seashells

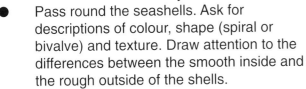

Learning objective
- To explore and show an interest in the texture of seashells

Preparation
- Mix grout with water if required.

What to do
Circle time
- Read *maggie and milly and molly and may.*
- Ask which children have been to the seaside for their holiday.
- Pass round the seashells. Ask for descriptions of colour, shape (spiral or bivalve) and texture. Draw attention to the differences between the smooth inside and the rough outside of the shells.

Craft activity
- Add a teaspoonful of paint to the grout and mix to a paste in a plastic pot.
- Spread over the tin, pot or lid. Keep the base clean.
- Press the seashells into the grout in a pleasing arrangement.

Extensions/variations
Art activity
- Make a collage from beach flotsam.
- Work with the children to create a large display of a beach scene. Help by suggesting appropriate materials and techniques.

Related activities
- Add water (see page 39)
- Storm (see page 40)
- Pebble pet (see page 95)

Resources
- Poem: *maggie and milly and molly and may* by e e cummings from *Verse Universe* (BBC Publications)
- Shells
- Grout
- Coloured powdered acrylic paint
- Teaspoon
- Spatula
- Plastic pot
- Flat-sided tin (CARE no sharp edges) or terracotta plant pot (plastic is too flexible) or circular cheese box with lid
- Dried beach flotsam
- Junk materials including fabric and string
- Paint
- Paintbrushes
- Coloured paper and tissue
- Cardboard
- PVA glue

Communication

(Seaside project)

• • • • • • • • • •

Resources

- Ring game: 'There's a Little Sandy Girl', from *This Little Puffin* compiled by Elizabeth Matterson (Puffin)
- Song: 'Heat Wave' by Irving Berlin (1888–1989)
- Song: 'We're All Going on a Summer Holiday' sung by Cliff Richard
- Song: 'Surfin' USA' by The Beach Boys
- Internet: search for 'song seaside' and select www.melodylane.net
- Song: 'Oh I Do Like to Be Beside the Seaside' by John A. Glover-Kind (19th century) American songwriter
- CD player or tape recorder

Learning objectives

- To enjoy joining in with ring games
- To create movement in response to music

Preparation

- Find the website.

What to do

Music activity

- Learn the ring game 'There's a Little Sandy Girl'.
- Play 'Heat Wave', and ask the children to act as though they are very hot.
- Play 'Surfin' USA' and ask the children to pretend that they are playing in the sea (explain what surfing is).
- Dance to 'We're All Going on a Summer Holiday' as a performance with the activity The beach (see page 162).

Extension/variation

Computer activity

- Look at the website which shows postcards of Victorian seaside holidays. Teach the words of the song 'Oh I Do Like to Be Beside the Seaside'.

Related activity

- Today's weather (see page 72)

Class

The beach

Class

Learning objective
● To use their imagination and pretend that they are at the seaside

Preparation
● Make ice lollies.

What to do

Circle time
● Ask the children where they went for their holiday away from home.
● Read *The Bears Who Went to the Seaside*. Ask what the bears took with them to use at the seaside. What did the bears do at the seaside?
● Ask them what they would take to the seaside. Make a list together.

Imaginative play activity
● Make a small beach by spreading clean sand over the grass (put a sheet of plastic down first).
● Borrow a small paddling pool. Let the children wear bathing costumes.
● Be involved in the children's imaginative play by pretending that the sea is at the edge of the sand.
● Share the ice lollies.

Extensions/variations
● Play beach games.
● Read 'The Picnic'. Talk about the problems of eating on a sandy beach.

Links to home
● Ask parents to remind their child of the holiday that they had.
● Tell parents about the project and ask for help to make a beach.
● Remind parents to bring child's swimming costume, towel, hat and sun screen.

Related activities
● Messing about in boats (see page 99)
● Silly balloons (see page 153)

Resources
■ Book: *The Bears Who Went to the Seaside* by Susanna Gretz and Alison Sage (A & C Black)
■ Easel or flip chart, felt-tip pen (optional)
■ Clean sand and plastic sheet
■ Buckets, spades, moulds to make patterns
■ Sticks to write in the sand
■ Seashells, small pieces of wood, pebbles
■ Beach toys
■ Small paddling pool
■ Poem: 'The Picnic' by Dorothy Aldis, from *Days Like This* compiled by Simon James (Walker Books)
■ Ice lolly moulds, diluted fruit juice, freezer

⚠ Supervise paddling pool activity closely.

Sandcastles

Resources
- Painting: *Children Playing on the Beach* by Mary Cassatt (1844–1926) – see *Looking at Paintings of Children* by Peggy Roalf (Belitha Press)
- Painting: *July, The Seaside* by L. S. Lowry (1887–1976)
- Poems: 'Seaside' and 'Sand', from *Out and About Through the Year* by Shirley Hughes (Walker Books)
- Wet sand tray
- Dry sand tray
- Seashells and pebbles
- Small buckets and spades

Learning objectives
- To capture experiences of the seaside with other materials or words
- To make comparisons between paintings of beach scenes

What to do

Circle time
- Ask the children if they have been to the seaside for their holiday.
- Read the poems 'Seaside' and 'Sand'. Which poem did you like the best?

Sand tray activity
- Suggest that the children make sandcastles. Talk about going to the beach.
- Ask which sand makes the best sandcastles.
- Ask about the texture of the wet and dry sand, seashells and pebbles.

Art activity
- Encourage the children to paint a picture of their holiday on the beach.
- Ask questions about their painting and how it relates to their holiday.

Extensions/variations
- Draw the children's attention to the composition of *Children Playing on the Beach* – the background is not clear, but you can see the blue sky, horizon, sea and sailing boats and the orange sandy beach. The children are making sandcastles.
- Compare with Shirley Hughes, illustration of the poem *Seaside* and with *July, The Seaside* by L. S. Lowry.

Related activity
- Pebble pet (see page 95)

Washing line

● ● ● ● ● ● ● ● ● ●

Learning objectives
● To draw and colour shapes of clothes
● To describe experiences in a variety of ways

Preparation
● Load program into computer if required.

What to do

Circle time
● Read the story *Doing the Washing.*
● How do you get the washing dry?
● Read the poem 'Clothes on the Washing Line'.

Art activity
● Support the children to draw and colour simple shapes of clothes. Talk about the colours of their clothes. Support language development: names of clothes and colours.
● Support cutting out the shapes and colour the reverse side with the same colour.
● Peg the shapes to a line hanging across the room.

Music activity
● Sing 'This is the Way We Wash Our Clothes' and learn the actions.

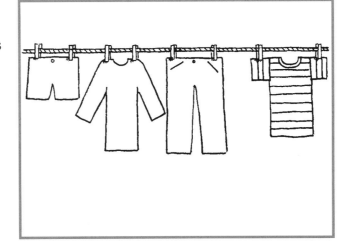

Extensions/variations
● Let the younger children colour in outlines of clothes.
● Use draw program on a computer to draw and fill shapes.

Links to home
● Ask parents to talk about the colours of their clothes.
● Ask parents to let their child help to hang up the washing, eg the children could hand the pegs over.

Related activity
● Coloured shapes (see page 20)

Resources
■ Book: *Doing the Washing* by Sarah Garland (Bodley Head Children's Books)
■ Poem: 'Clothes on the Washing Line' by Frank Flynn, from *The Oxford Treasury of Children's Poems* (Oxford University Press)
■ Paper and paints
■ Pegs and line
■ Song: 'This is the Way We Wash Our Clothes', from *This Little Puffin* compiled by Elizabeth Matterson (Puffin)
■ Computer with draw program, printer and paper
■ Scissors

● ● ● ● ● ● ● ● ● ●

 Supervise the use of scissors. Hang the line high enough not to be reached by the children.

Splish drip splosh

8

Communication
(Sorcerer's Apprentice project)
• • • • • • • • • •

Resources
- Poem: 'Water', from *Out and About Through the Year* by Shirley Hughes (Walker Books)
- Video: *STOMP Out Loud* (VCI)
- Whiteboard or flip board and pens
- Tape recorder
- Blank cassette tape
- Junk materials
- Purchased instruments
- Book for instruments to make: *The I Can't Sing Book* by Jackie Silberg (Brilliant Publications)
- Video recorder and television

Learning objective
- To make up sounds associated with water and use them to tap out simple repeated rhythms

Preparation
- Find the section in the video *STOMP Out Loud* when the performers are in the 'sewer'.

What to do
Book corner
- Read the poem 'Water' and talk about the sounds that are being made in the swimming baths and by the little girl playing with the water.

Circle time
- Show the video for ideas on how water can make sounds.
- Discuss the video and ask how the performers made different sounds.
- Ask for words associated with water. Support language development: *pour*, *freeze*, *trickle*, *splash*, *dribble*, *bubble*, etc.
- Write down the words with the name of the child who made the suggestion beside it.

Music activity
- Read the poem 'Water' and remind the children of the words.
- With the children working in pairs, encourage them to choose one of the words and make up sounds (using water if appropriate) with homemade and purchased instruments to represent it.

Extensions/variations
- Encourage one of the pair of children to say the appropriate word several times with expression in a beat, and the other child to add an appropriate sound accompaniment. For example, if the word chosen was 'bubble', the child might make bubbles by blowing with a straw in water.
- Record the children's work on the tape recorder.

Links to home
- Ask parents who take their child swimming to talk about the sounds that the water makes.

Related activities
- Rattle those pans (see page 51)
- Running water (see page 71)
- Under my umbrella (see page 102)

Too full

Communication
• • • • • • • • • •

6

Learning objective
- To engage in imaginative and role play based upon 'The Sorcerer's Apprentice'

Preparation
- Find section on *Fantasia* video.

What to do
Circle time
- Watch 'The Sorcerer's Apprentice'.
- Ask what went wrong? What happened when the apprentice (Mickey) chopped up the broom?
- What do you think the Sorcerer had to say?
- How did Mickey show he was sorry?
- Ask the children to imagine what would happen if they had to do the washing up, and they made the dishes wash themselves, then it all went wrong.

Water tray activity
- Ask the children to find out how many small pots full of water will fill the large container. Suggest using a new small container each time to keep count.
- Observe whether the children include in their play what they have seen on the video.
- Support language development: *full*, *overflow*, *half full*, *empty*, *container*.

Extensions/variations
- Use the sand tray instead of the water tray.
- Make a hole in one of the containers and sing 'There's a Hole in My Bucket'.

Resources
- Video: 'The Sorcerer's Apprentice' by Paul Dukas (1865–1935) in *Fantasia* (Walt Disney)
- Video recorder and television
- Water tray
- Plenty of small yoghurt pots
- One larger container
- Washing-up bowl
- Plastic plates
- Empty washing-up liquid bottle
- Sponge or cloth
- Dry sand tray
- Song: 'There's a Hole in My Bucket', see www.kididdles.com

• • • • • • • • • •

 Supervise water tray.

The Sorcerer's Apprentice

Communication

(Sorcerer's Apprentice project)

• • • • • • • • • •

Resources
- Video: 'The Sorcerer's Apprentice' by Paul Dukas (1865–1935) in *Fantasia* (Walt Disney)
- Video recorder and television
- Resources as requested

Learning objectives
- To express and communicate their ideas, thoughts and feelings about the story of 'The Sorcerer's Apprentice' by choosing to use a widening range of materials, suitable tools, imaginative and role play, designing and making, and musical instruments
- To talk about personal intentions, describing what they were trying to do
- To respond to comments and questions, entering into dialogue about their creations

Preparation
- The children should have attempted the previous activities in this project.

What to do
Circle time
- Watch the video 'The Sorcerer's Apprentice'.
- Suggest that the children choose an activity they wish to improve upon, or one they have not done, eg painting a picture, designing and making a sorcerer's hat, making buckets, making up a dance to the music.

Extensions/variations
Show and tell
- Let the children show and explain their work to the group, stating which activity they preferred.
- Encourage the group to talk about each other's work in positive terms.

Related activities
- Tooth fairy beads (see pages 28–29) for playdough
- Myself (see page 31) for papier-mâché
- Hats (see pages 32–33)

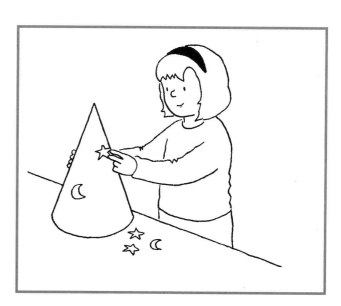

Icicles

(2)

Learning objectives
- To explore colour, texture, shape, form and space in two dimensions using a computer to assist the design
- To mix media in a collage

Preparation
- Load the draw program on to the computer.

What to do

Art activity
- Ask what shape the children think of when they feel cold. Have they ever seen icicles?
- Encourage the children to draw 'spiky' shapes on to cardboard, then connect them so the card looks like a jigsaw. The design could be made with a draw program on the computer.
- Cut out the shapes and cover some with fabric and threads. Paint some of the shapes.
- Stick the shapes back together like a jigsaw.
- Encourage the children to talk about what they are making.

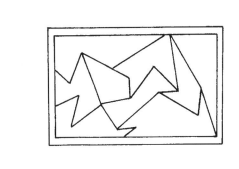

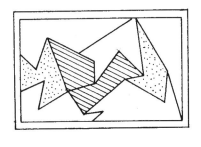

Related activity
- Washing line (see page 164)

Resources
- Computer with draw program, printer and paper
- Fabrics and threads
- Cardboard
- PVA glue and spreaders
- Stiff paper
- Paints
- Paintbrushes
- Scissors

 Supervise the use of scissors.

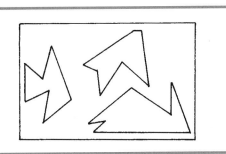

© Mavis Brown
www.brilliantpublications.co.uk

Getting colder

Communication

(Freezing cold project)

• • • • • • • • • •

Resources

- Poem: 'Cold', from *Out and About Through the Year* by Shirley Hughes (Walker Books)
- Songs: 'The North Wind Doth Blow' and 'Here We Go Round the Mulberry Bush', from *This Little Puffin* compiled by Elizabeth Matterson (Puffin)
- Song: 'It's a Cold Day', from *Start with a Song* by Mavis de Mierre (Brilliant Publications)
- Dressing-up box for clothes for cold weather

Learning objectives

- To join in with songs and begin to build a repertoire of favourite songs
- To make up simple songs and mime feeling cold

What to do

Circle time

- Read the poem 'Cold' and show the illustrations.
- Ask the children to describe how they felt when it was cold weather.
- Ask them to show you what they do when they feel cold. Do they put on warmer clothes? Flap their arms, etc?

Music activity

- Learn and sing 'The North Wind Doth Blow'.
- Ask them to pretend to shiver like the cold robin.
- Sing 'Here We Go Round the Mulberry Bush' and do the actions.

Role play activity

- Encourage the children to dress up for cold weather.
- Support language development: *cold*, *chilly*, *freezing*, *icy*.

Extensions/variations

- Sing 'It's a Cold Day' and do the actions.
- Encourage the children to add more verses, eg flap arms, put on gloves.

Related activities

- Time to go home (see page 19)
- Today's weather (see page 72)

Class

South Pole

Learning objective

- To use their imagination in music and dance by matching movements to orchestral music that describes icy weather

Preparation

- Listen to the CD to find the relevant part of the music (2 minutes after the beginning). In the second movement of the 'Prelude' the soprano begins to sing and a wind machine can be heard. The music begins to swirl into a crescendo.

What to do

Circle time

- Ask the children whether they have been outside in a snowstorm.
- Ask them how they would walk. Would they hold on to their hat or scarf or hug themselves to try to keep warm? Would they shiver?
- Tell the children that this piece of music was written for a film called *Scott of the Antarctic*.
- Listen to the music. Ask the children what kind of place the Antarctic would be. Do they think it would be hot or cold? Would it be safe or dangerous?
- Then tell the children it was very cold and dangerous with nothing but ice, snow and wind. Show photographs.

Dance activity

- Ask the children to pretend that they are in a snowstorm. Encourage them to mime pushing against the cold wind.
- Suggest that they be the wind, and mime how it swirls around.
- Play the music and ask them to move to the music this time.
- Ask individual children to demonstrate to the group, then ask why their movements matched the music. (Fast music/fast movement/swirling snow.)

Extension/variation

- Divide the class into two groups, with one acting as though they are walking against the wind, and the other as though they are the wind. Make the rule that there should be no contact with each other.

Related activities

- The Selfish Giant project (see pages 145–150)

Resources

- Music: 'Prelude (Andante Maestoso)', from *Sinfonia Antartica* by Ralph Vaughan Williams (1872–1958)
- Book or photographs showing the Antarctic (continent at the South Pole)
- CD player

Freezing

Communication

(Freezing cold project)

• • • • • • • • •

Resources

- Blocks of ice
- Poem: 'Ice' by Walter de la Mare from *The Oxford Treasury of Children's Poems* (Oxford University Press)
- Painting: *Cold Mountain 6 (Bridge)* by Brice Marden (b.1938)
- Paints
- Paintbrushes
- White, blue, black paper
- Glue and glue spreaders
- Fabrics and threads
- Cardboard
- Stiff paper
- Scissors
- String

• • • • • • • • • •

 Do not use ice straight out of the freezer. Let it warm up first. Supervise the use of scissors.

Learning objective

- Express and communicate their ideas and thoughts about feeling cold

What to do

Circle time

- Pass round the small block of ice.
- Ask the children to describe its texture and how they feel touching the ice.
- Read the poem 'Ice'. Ask if the poem is a good description of ice.

Art activity

- Look at and discuss the painting *Cold Mountain 6 (Bridge)*. It shows grey and black curved lines and evokes how the artist felt as he looked at the mountain.
- Ask the children to compose a picture, using a range of materials, of how they would feel (not look like) in an icy storm.
- Encourage the children to talk about their work.

Extension/variation

- Encourage the children to make up a story or poem about being cold.

Related activities

- Add water (see page 39)
- Storm (see page 40)

Useful addresses

Aerial photographs of school as posters and playmats, weather symbols, etc
Wildgoose
The Old Toy Factory
10 The Business Park
Jackson Street
Coalville
Leicestershire LE67 3NR
www.wgoose.co.uk

Air dry Model Magic
www.crayola.com

Be Safe! Health and safety in primary school science and technology (3rd edition)
Association of Science Education
College Lane
Hatfield
Hertfordshire AL10 9AA

Binca cloth
Galt Educational and Pre-School
Johnsonbrook Road
Hyde
Cheshire SK14 4QT

British Toy Museums near you
www.toy.co.uk

Children's songs (with words and music)
www.kididdles.com

Computer software
2Simple Software
3–4 Sentinel Square
Brent Street
Hendon NW4 2EL
www.2simplesoftware.com

Dorling Kindersley CD-ROMs
GSP Ltd
Meadow Lane
St Ives
Cambridgeshire PE27 4LG

For Weather Teddy
Granada Learning
Granada Television
Quay Street
Manchester M60 9EA
www.granada-learning.com

Designing and Making supplies
S&S Services
3 Kinwarton Workshops
Arden Forest Industrial Estate
Alchester
Warwickshire B49 6EH
www.ss-services.co.uk

Early years pretend play, water and sand trays; multicultural art posters; finger puppets
NES Arnold
General enquiries
Novara House
Excelsior Road
Ashby Park
Ashby-de-la-Zouch
Leicestershire LE65 1NG

Fabric crayons, paints, etc
Berol
Sanford UK Ltd
Oldmedow Road
King's Lynn
Norfolk PE30 4JR
www.sanford.co.uk

Modelling clay
Hope Education
Hyde Buildings
Aston Road
Hyde
Chesire
SK14 4JH
www.hope-education.co.uk

Multicultural play food; baby dolls; puppets; puzzles and card games
EDUZONE
3 Dennis Parade
Winchmore Hill Road
London N14 6AA

Music; Musicals
International Music Publications Ltd (IMP)
Griffin House
161 Hammersmith Road
London W6 8BS

Musical instruments; world music
Music Educational Supplies Ltd (MES)
101 Banstead Road South
Sutton
Surrey SM2 5LH

Posters
PCET Publishing
27 Kirchen Road
London W13 0UD
www.pcet.co.uk

Glossary of terms

abstract
A picture reduced to its essential visual elements (eg lines, shapes, colours)

acoustic
Non-electronic means of sound production (as in acoustic instruments)

aesthetic
Relates to what is considered to be beautiful or artistic

armature
A frame supporting a 3D sculpture

beat
The regular pulse of music

body percussion
A percussive sound created using the body (eg stomp, pat, clap, snap)

choreography
Planning and arranging dance movements into a finished dance work

closed sounds
Sound is dull and short, eg a triangle held by the hand to stop it vibrating

collage
2D image created by gluing materials such as paper and fabric scraps to a flat surface

context
Circumstances influencing the creation of the work, such as intention, time and place, eg skipping songs

cool down
After activity, to help children's heart rates return to normal and to help them become still

dance drama
Individual or group drama based on movements that tell a story, with music as either stimulus or accompaniment

duration
Long or short rhythmic patterns

dynamics
In music, the degree of loudness or softness, ie volume; in dance, one of the five elements of movement; refers to how the body is moving

found instruments
Everyday objects used as classroom instruments to create music (eg PVC piping, pots and pans, kitchen utensils)

found objects
Everyday objects recycled or incorporated into an artwork

found sounds
Body sounds, found instruments, traditional instruments, voices, natural sounds, synthetic sounds to create a music composition (see soundscape)

graphics
2D images produced by processes such as printmaking, photography, and computer graphic applications

harmony
The combination of pitched notes in a way that is musically significant

installation
A 3D arrangement often constructed of found objects and involving mixed media

logo
A symbolic design to identify an organization

maquette
A small sculpture made as a trial or sketch for a larger piece

melody
The arrangement and sequence of pitches

MIDI
Musical Instrument Digital Interface – standard specifications that enable electronic instruments such as synthesizers, samplers, sequencers, or drum machines to communicate with one another and with computers

monoprint
Printing by transferring a painted design on to paper by laying the paper over the painted surface; only one print can be made of each design

narrative
Follows a story line

open sounds
When the sound is bright and resonates by using a metal beater and allowing the instrument to vibrate

Orff instruments
A set of barred instruments (glockenspiels, metallophones, and xylophones) for teaching music

ostinato (plural ostinati)
A rhythmic or melodic pattern that is repeated persistently throughout a composition

pattern
Repetition of one or more of the elements in a planned way, eg a sequence of three different movements, shapes and colours, or verse followed by chorus

percussion instrument
Any instrument that is played by striking, shaking or scraping

performance
A production of dance, drama or music for an audience

personal space
The 'space bubble' that a dancer occupies, including all levels, planes, and directions both near to and far from the body's centre

pitch
High and low notes (result of many or few vibrations)

poster
A sign used to advertise a simple message

programme music
Music inspired by a story or visual image, eg *Peer Gynt suite*, *Carnival of the Animals*, *Peter and the Wolf* (also known as illustrative music)

repertoire
Music and dance learned, performed or listened to

rhythm
In music, the arrangement of notes and silences of varying duration; the beat may be slow, but each note having a short duration results in a running rhythm

round
The same melody sung by two or more parts, beginning one after another; all parts sing at the same pitch

solfa
Notation that uses syllabic names (do, re, mi, fa, so, la, ti, do) to represent the notes of the scale relative to the tonic

soundscape
A free-form composition using any arrangement or ordering of sounds and any combination of traditional instruments, non-traditional instruments, voices, body percussion, natural sounds, found sounds, synthetic sounds, technology, and so on

style
A distinctive quality given to a creation by its creator or performer, eg ballet and the lambada are styles of dance

tempo
Slower and faster beats; a brisk march has a faster tempo than a slow waltz

timbre
The characteristic or quality of the sound that distinguishes one instrument, voice or sound source from another, eg a clarinet can be distinguished from a horn

vocables
The voice is used as an instrument as opposed to singing words

warm up
Before physical activity, a series of movements and exercises to prepare the body

© Mavis Brown
www.brilliantpublications.co.uk

Topic index

© Mavis Brown

www.brilliantpublications.co.uk